NEW SWEDEN

ON THE DELAWARE

NEW SWEDEN ON THE DELAWARE
A Photographic Tour of the Historic Sites of America's First Swedes and Finns

Library of Congress Control Number: 2013934582

International Standard Book Number: 978-0-9762501-6-6

Design layout by Cataleno & Co., Inc., Moorestown, New Jersey
Printed in the U.S.A. by Thomson-Shore, Inc., Dexter, Michigan

The Swedish Colonial Society
916 South Swanson Street
Philadelphia, Pennsylvania 19147-4332
info@colonialswedes.org

Visit us on the web at:
www.ColonialSwedes.org

NEW SWEDEN

ON THE DELAWARE

A PHOTOGRAPHIC TOUR OF THE HISTORIC SITES OF
AMERICA'S FIRST SWEDES AND FINNS

PHOTOGRAPHY BY KENNETH S. PETERSON
TEXT BY KIM-ERIC WILLIAMS
EDITED BY RONALD A. HENDRICKSON

THE SWEDISH COLONIAL SOCIETY
PHILADELPHIA, PENNSYLVANIA

dedication

This book is dedicated to the colonial ancestors who came to the New Sweden Colony on the Delaware River from 1638-1783. These Forefathers and Foremothers came mostly from Sweden and Finland and carved out a new life in an unknown land. The first test of their fortitude was the four-six month voyage in small wooden sailing ships with inadequate sanitation and food. It is no wonder that they declared the first piece of sighted land in the Delaware Bay as "Paradise Point." This new land wafted its arboreal sweetness on the breezes even before they could actually see it on the horizon. They remained on the land even when the majority language was no longer Swedish but became Dutch or English.

The pictures in this volume remind us of part of what they accomplished, but they do not begin to cover the expansion of these immigrant families all over the 50 states. Today their descendants number between 10 and 20 million citizens, many more than the descendants of the Great Swedish Immigration of the 19th century. Most of those whose forbearers came to New Sweden are unaware of their own genealogy, since it involves tracing one's ancestors back more than 10 generations. The Swedish Colonial Society and its website, *ColonialSwedes.org* are ready to assist anyone who suspects that this story may be their own story. It is our hope that these glimpses of *New Sweden on the Delaware* will whet your appetite, expand your knowledge and encourage your curiosity.

A Guide to New Sweden Forefathers is on pages 118-121.

contents

Foreword by His Excellency Jonas Hafström   8
Foreword by Her Excellency Ritva Koukku-Ronde   9
Introduction   11
Land of the Lenape   13

delaware

Delaware map   14
Delaware introduction   15
Kalmar Nyckel   17
New Sweden Centre   18
Timen Stiddem Old Barley Mill Site   19
Fort Christina Park   20
Holy Trinity (Old Swedes') Church   22
Hendrickson House   26
Crane Hook Church Monument & Marker   28
Wertmüller House   29
New Castle   30

pennsylvania

Pennsylvania introduction   33
Pennsylvania map   34
Governor Printz Park   36
Gloria Dei (Old Swedes') Church   39
American Swedish Historical Museum   42
Philadephia City Hall Statues   46
Old Swedish Burial Ground   48
Monument to Finnish Settlers   49
Morton Homestead   50
Morton Morton House   52
Calcon Hook   53
Techoherassi: Olof Stille Site   54
Lower Swedish Log Cabin   57
St. James Church of Kingsessing   58
Bartram's Garden   60
Printz's (Old Swedes') Mill at Cobbs Creek   63
Christ Church Upper Merion   64
St. Gabriel's Episcopal Church   66
Mouns Jones House   68
Brossman Center   69

new jersey

New Jersey map	70
New Jersey introduction	71
Fort Elfsborg	73
Trinity Episcopal (Old Swedes') Church	74
Schorn Log Cabin	77
Mullica House	78
C.A. Nothnagle Log House	80
St. George's Episcopal (Old Swedes') Church	83
New Sweden Heritage Monument	84
Johan Printz Park Log Cabin	85
Tyler (Hancock) Log House	86
New Sweden Colonial Farmstead Museum & Living History Center	88
Swedish Granary	89
Moravian Church on Oldman's Creek	90
Moravian Church Site on Maurice River	91
Caesar Hoskins Log Cabin	92
Steelman (Stille) Family Cemetery	93

maryland and washington, d.c.

Maryland & Washington, D.C., map	94
Maryland & Washington, D.C., introduction	95
St. Mary Anne's Episcopal Church	96
Coon's Log Cabin	99
John Hans Steelman House/Historic Elk Landing	100
Embassy of Sweden	102
Embassy of Finland	106
The First Hundred Years of the Swedish Colonial Society	110
Governors of the Swedish Colonial Society (1909-present)	115
Publications of the Swedish Colonial Society	116
A Guide to New Sweden Forefathers (1638-1664 Arrivals)	118
Index	122
About the Authors and Artists	126

foreword

When the New World beckoned, adventurous Swedes were among the first to board ships to settle this new frontier and, in 1638, the original *Kalmar Nyckel* sailed up the Delaware River.

My countrymen have been venturing out into the world since the late eighth century. Sweden has benefitted from the contacts and the exchange of knowledge and ideas brought back from foreign cultures. And our relationship with America has been especially rich and successful.

Swedish Americans fought in the Revolutionary War. John Morton, of Swedish heritage, signed the Declaration of Independence. Swedish Americans fought in the War Between the States, as it is called down south. The ironclad *Monitor*, which helped to turn the direction of the war, was designed by Swedish inventor John Ericsson.

Swedish farmers helped to cultivate the Midwest, which in turn permitted the rest of the country to thrive. Swedish entrepreneurs built vast networks of travel bureaus, hotels, department stores, small jewelry boutiques, bakeries and media outlets.

Today, Sweden and the United States enjoy great relations and have a steady exchange of ideas in the areas of trade, entrepreneurship, education, scientific research, climate change and foreign policy. Alfred Nobel (inventor whose legacy lives on in the annual Nobel Prizes), Raoul Wallenberg (humanitarian and rescuer), Astrid Lindgren (author and mother of Pippi Longstocking), Marcus Samuelson (chef and restaurateur), Robyn (one of many singer/songwriters following ABBA), Pia Sundhagen (soccer coach led American team to London Olympics gold), Annika Sorenstam (golfer superior) and Stieg Larsson (*Millennium* trilogy author) are some Swedes who made names for themselves in America. These very different persons embody well-known traits of Swedes: benevolent, creative, innovative and acutely aware of the world around them. But they have each expressed themselves in very disparate manners.

The Swedes who settled in the Delaware Valley 375 years ago were clever, sturdy folks who were quite aware of the need to befriend the natives who greeted them if they were to survive the harsh winters in their new homeland.

Survive they did.

And Swedes have succeeded in living harmoniously on this continent ever since, contributing to the American history, society and future through their compassion, creativity and hard work.

Jonas Hafström
Ambassador of Sweden to the United States of America

foreword

In 2013 we are celebrating the 375th anniversary of the arrival of two tall ships – the *Kalmar Nyckel* and the *Fogel Grip* – to North America on 28 March 1638. The captain was a Dutchman, Peter Minuit, but his crew consisted of Finns and Swedes who came to explore the new continent. Finland was at that time under Swedish rule, and many of the Finns onboard had first moved to Sweden and then continued their journey to America. These Finns and Swedes who arrived in the present-day Wilmington, Delaware, liked what they found and established a successful colony.

Today there are approximately 750,000 Finns or Americans with Finnish heritage living in the United States. When you add all the people linked to Finland through friends, family, coworkers or neighbors, this number skyrockets.

Since the days of *Kalmar Nyckel* and *Fogel Grip*, Finland has developed from a timber and agriculture–based economy to a modern, technology-based one. Through stories and photographs, this book *New Sweden on the Delaware* brings modern Finland and Sweden nicely together with historic and contemporary America. It is wonderful to see how beautifully the log cabin tradition that the Finns brought to the United States and have been especially good at since we have always had a close relationship with the forests, is displayed in the book.

I would like to take this opportunity to thank the Swedish Colonial Society for its invaluable work for all the friends of Nordic culture by bringing them this wonderful collection of photographs depicting the history of both Finland and Sweden in the United States. I am truly happy to see how the Society is committed to creating a broader community of all Swedish and Finnish Americans, as well as Swedish and Finnish citizens living in America, and other Americans.

I congratulate the Swedish Colonial Society for its great input into organizing the celebrations of Swedish American and Finnish American culture and heritage during this year of the 375th anniversary.

I am also sure all of you, dear readers and friends of Finnish and Swedish culture, will help continue the important work in community building and remembering our heritage in the United States for years to come. I am looking forward to our countries deepening our relationship even further with the help of our long history together.

Ritva Koukku-Ronde

Ambassador of Finland to the United States of America

introduction

Not enough Americans know that Sweden had a colony here in the Delaware Valley in the early 17th century. Those Swedish and Finnish colonists and soldiers arrived here decades before William Penn and his Quakers. Their descendants are all over the Delaware Valley and beyond. Some of their customs became a part of the American culture and they likewise borrowed traits from those around them, as you will notice in these photographs.

My collection of photographs began as a personal quest to locate and photograph all remaining Swedish and Finnish historical sites and monuments. Upon donating the photos to the Swedish Colonial Society I was surprised by the call to have them published by Dr. Peter S. Craig and enthusiastically seconded by the Council.

Many people have shown their support and worked hard to make this publication a reality. We wish to thank the Swedish Council of America for their generous financial support. This work came about because of the generosity and sacrifice of Ronald and Nancy Hendrickson of Cataleno & Company. Much appreciation goes to the Rev. Dr. Kim-Eric Williams for writing the entire text. He, too, believed in this project from the beginning. Finally, many thanks to Governor Sally Bridwell, James and Doriney Seagers, Aleasa Hogate, Rev. David Anderson, Ellen Rye, Earl and Sylvia Seppala, Herbert Rambo and the entire Council of the Swedish Colonial Society.

I hope you are inspired and learn something new from this fresh view of New Sweden.

Kenneth S. Peterson

land of the lenape

The Lenape (len-ah'-pee) people have inhabited the Delaware Valley since about 10,000 B.C. Their name means "Real People" and since "Lenni" also means "real" it is not appropriate to use it as a prefix. Because of wars with their neighbors, their population had been reduced to about 10,000 when the New Sweden Colony was established in 1638. In Lenapehocking, the Land of the Lenape, they were spread out in some 40 villages. This was a rather sparse settlement and was no doubt an attraction for Peter Minuit in planning where Ft. Christina should be placed.

The Lenape south of the Raritan River spoke an Unami dialect that differed from those of the Munsi region to the north. They were a part of the six large Algonquin nations in the Northeast. While Lenape still reside in the Delaware Valley, many of them moved to Ontario or Oklahoma, as Europeans expropriated their lands.

The relationship with the Lenape was on the whole peaceful and mutually beneficial. The Europeans would have starved to death without the possibility of purchasing corn from the Indians. Since the Indians had no metallurgy, they found axes, hoes, and pots to be extremely useful. While the relationship was strained by the paucity of trade goods that the Swedes had to offer, owing to the few ships that came from Sweden, personal ties developed that were satisfying to everyone. Unlike the Dutch and English, the New Sweden settlers were used to the forests. They could go hunting or fishing together. They even shared a common agricultural methodology, especially the Forest Finns who had brought slash and burn agriculture to a superior level of development. They could even share the sweat lodge, although the Europeans called it a sauna or bastu.

The Lenape clearly distinguished between the New Sweden settlers and the other Europeans on the East Coast. They called the Swedes and Finns, *Koores*, while the Dutch, English and Germans were *Senoares*. In the few cases where violence broke out the Swedish Governors used traditional Lenape law to settle the dispute. In fact, the Lenape and the New Sweden people got along so well that their relationship was a singular example of co-existence.

Wilmington Area
enlarged behind inset

Pennsylvania

Maryland

Delaware

New Jersey

Delaware
River

Brandywine
Creek

Christina River

Christina
Park

Swedes Landing Rd

E 7th St

E 6th St

Lord St

E 4th St

N Church St

E 7th St

① Kalmar Nyckel
② New Sweden Centre
③ Fort Christina State Park
④ Holy Trinity (Old Swedes') Church
⑤ Hendrickson House &
    Crane Hook Church Monument

⑥ Timen Stiddem Old Barley Mill Site
⑦ Crane Hook Church Marker
⑧ Wertmüller House
⑨ New Castle

delaware

Often called the "First State" since it was the first of the 13 to ratify the Constitution, it is also the site of the first European settlement in the area. While Swedish King Gustavus Adolphus (Gustaf II Adolf) had shown interest in several foreign trading companies from 1624 until his death in battle in 1632, it was not until 1636 that the New Sweden Company was founded. Led by Peter Minuit, former Governor of New Netherland, and supported by various Dutch and Swedish investors, two ships, the *Kalmar Nyckel* (Key of Kalmar) and *Fogel Grip* (Bird Griffen) left Gothenburg harbor at the beginning of November 1637. They arrived in the Minquis (Christina) River on April 8, (March 29, OS) 1638 and anchored at a known natural rocky landing place. The location was deliberately chosen by Minuit who had traveled on the South (Delaware) River several times. It was hidden from other European traders and was convenient to trade with the local Lenape people.

After the expedition met the local Indians and signed deeds of friendship and settlement, 24 military men of the group led in the construction of Ft. Christina near the Rocks where they had initially landed. The object of the Company was to make money for the investors by buying furs and tobacco from the Lenape. It was not seen as a permanent settlement, since Sweden had no excess population and relatively little poverty. The settlers who came later stayed mostly in the northern part of the state, few going further south than New Castle. Although the three "Lower Counties" were not at first granted to William Penn, he later obtained them to protect access to Philadelphia. They were separately administered from New Castle by 1700 because of the difficulties of traveling to Philadelphia for the Provincial Assembly. This gave this area an identity that was distinct from Pennsylvania, from which it broke away during the Revolution. In 1731 Thomas Willing founded Willingtown as a Quaker settlement above Ft. Christina and eventually that city and Christina merged and became known as Wilmington.

[1]

[2]

Kalmar Nyckel

The replica ship **Kalmar Nyckel** [1] (Key of Kalmar) was originally envisioned in 1938 but was not launched until 1998, when it was built under the auspices of the Kalmar Nyckel Foundation at the 7th Street Shipyard near the Rocks. The original ship, a pinance, was built in the Netherlands and was named for the strategic castle and fort in the city of Kalmar on the Baltic coast. This grand defense was for many years the "key" to Sweden's southern boundary with Denmark. In all, 13 different voyages set out from Gothenburg and 11 reached their new world destination. The *Kalmar Nyckel* led four of them successfully. The **artfully hand carved stern** [2] is typical of ships of the time and in this version we see some familiar faces of people who were instrumental in the building of the ship.

As the State of Delaware's "Tall Ship" the *Kalmar Nyckel* regularly travels to New Castle and Lewes and in the summers from Norfolk, Virginia to Provincetown, Massachusetts. Volunteer crews and expert mates and captains learn again the joys, hardships and maneuvers of 17th century sailing.

Visitor Information

To visit the shipyard, reserve a spot on a sailing event or to arrange a private charter sail, call the Kalmar Nyckel Foundation at 302-429-7447, or visit the web site: kalmarnyckel.org.

Kalmar Nyckel Foundation
1124 East 7th Street, Wilmington, DE 19801
phone: 302-429-7447
email: info@kalmarnyckel.org
web: kalmarnyckel.org

New Sweden Centre

The New Sweden Centre is a "hands-on" museum at the Kalmar Nyckel Shipyard that began in 1987 as the Kalmar Nyckel Museum Institute. Its purpose is to inform visitors to the Seventh Street peninsula about colonial history. Founded by Malcolm L. Mackenzie, civic activist and historian who initially proposed the rebuilding of the Kalmar Nyckel and was the long-time Recording Secretary of the Swedish Colonial Society, it is now housed in a former blacksmith's shop and features a small but fascinating exhibition entitled "Experience New Sweden."

Visitor Information

Tours & visits are by appointment. Please call 302-429-0464 to schedule.

New Sweden Centre
1124 East 7th Street, Wilmington, DE 19801
phone: 302-429-0464
email: info@colonialnewsweden.org
web: colonialnewsweden.org

Timen Stiddem Old Barley Mill Site

Timen Stiddem, the famed barber-surgeon of the New Sweden Company and the first medical doctor in Delaware, owned a mill at this site after 1671. This was the location of the first mill on the Brandywine – a corruption of the Swedish word, brännvin, which means "burning wine" – a very popular vodka-like intoxicant that needed the fresh waters of this stream plus barley. Today, it is usually called aqua vit. The same stream provided power for the flourmills and the DuPont gunpowder mills that made Wilmington economically successful.

Visitor Information

The mill site is located in Brandywine Park, which is open 8:00 a.m. to sunset.

Timen Stiddem Old Barley Mill Site

Brandywine Park

N. Adams St. at S. Park Dr., Wilmington, DE 19802

phone: 302-577-7020

web: destateparks.com/park/wilmington/brandywine-park

    or

       homepages.rootsweb.ancestry.com/~stiddem/

       photos-htm/1-mill.htm

OLD MILL STONE

NEAR THIS SITE
THE FIRST GRIST MILL
WAS BUILT ABOUT 1640
BY
ASHMOND STIDHAM

IT WAS HERE THAT THE
"OLD BARLEY MILL"
WAS BUILT IN 1765

THIS STONE IS THE LONE RELIC
OF THESE
VANISHED MILLS

Fort Christina Park

This shoebox park was created by the State of Delaware in 1938 to protect what was still remaining of the original "Rocks" landing site of 1638. Since no archeological excavations have ever been undertaken, it is not certain exactly where the original fort was sited. Some of it probably exceeded the narrow bounds of the present park. The Swedish **granite monolith [1]** was a gift from Sweden in 1938 and was created by famed sculptor Carl Milles (1875-1955). Funds had been raised by radio announcements all over Sweden known as the "10 Öre Collection." It shows a stylized *Kalmar Nyckel* at the top and various colonial scenes, including a humorous version of **Governor Johan Printz [2]** greeting Indians who sport Sioux war bonnets instead of the more modest Lenape headwear. The

[2]

[1]

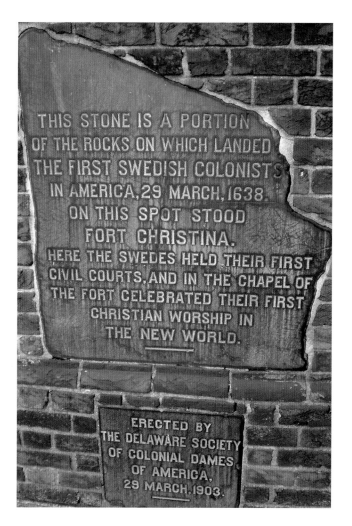

June 27th dedication was honored by a delegation of 80 people from Sweden, coming by boat and led by Crown Prince Gustaf Adolf and Prince Bertil. President Franklin Delano Roosevelt accepted the monument on behalf of the American people and alluded to his own Swedish ancestors – he was an Honorary Forefather member of the Swedish Colonial Society. Excessive rain darkened the day but not the spirits of the large crowd. A copy of this monument is on the old stone wharf in Gothenburg, Sweden. In the park was the 18th century Stalcop-Fenimore log cabin that formerly stood at Price's Corner. It was moved here in 1957 to illustrate the introduction of the log cabin to America, but was removed in 2013. A **state marker [3]** for Black Anthony, the first African settler in New Sweden – a free Black from Angola – stands nearby.

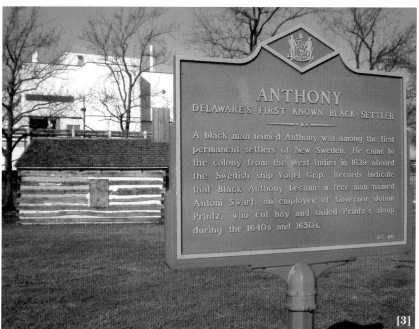

Visitor Information

To visit the park, contact the Delaware Division of Historical & Cultural Affairs at 302-736-7400, or visit the web site: history.delaware.gov.

Fort Christina State Park

1110 East 7th Street
    Wilmington, DE 19801
phone: 302-736-7400
web: history.delaware.gov

Holy Trinity (Old Swedes') Church

It is assumed that Pastor Torkil Reorus (1640-1643) conducted Lutheran church services in Ft. Christina as early as 1640. This site was disallowed when the Dutch captured the colony in 1655 and the Swedes were forced to meet in homes until 1667, when they were able to erect a log church at Crane Hook on the south side of the Christina River with help of Pastor Lars Carlson Lock, the only priest to remain after the Dutch took control of the colony in 1655. In 1697 the Church of Sweden sent three priests to renew the work of the American mission and one of these, Erik Björk, led the congregation to move across the river and in 1698-1699 build the present granite church near Ft. Christina. It was dedicated on Holy Trinity Sunday, July 4, 1699. Its design is typical of medieval stone churches in Sweden, although the

[4]

charming and non-matching **brick tower [1]** was added in 1802. The original black walnut **pulpit [2]** stands in its original position. The **dove [3]** above the preacher's head is a gift from Sweden and symbolizes the Holy Spirit with whose power the Word is proclaimed. The pews were restored according to original drawings in 1899. The **stained glass [9]** came at the end of the 19th century and the present free-standing **altar [2]** is the newest addition to the chancel. Ancient **graffiti [4]** exposed in a late 20th century restoration of the **south porch [5]** doors was left exposed. In 1830 a new Trinity Chapel was built at King and Fifth Streets to serve the growing city

[3]

[2]

and again in 1891 the parish dedicated a very large Gothic Church at Adams Street and Delaware Avenue. It continues today as one parish with two worship locations.

Oil portraits of Pastors **Erik Björk [6]** (1697-1713), Peter Tranberg (1741-1748) and Israel Acrelius (1749-1756) are treasured possessions of the church. The **grave of Pastor Tranberg [7]** is located at the head of the center aisle. The grave of the infant son of Pastor Lars Girelius (1768-1791) the last priest of the Church of Sweden to serve the

Wid Christina i Pennsil I 17 åhr. Til Fahlun åhr 1714. Then 5 i ordningen Kyrçkoh:och Probst vid Fahlun.

[6]

church is also in the nave. The grave of Charles Springer, who wrote the letter to the King of Sweden, including a census of all the Swedes on the Delaware in 1693, and longtime Warden and Lay reader, is at the south portico. In the large cemetery are buried members of the Bayard, Vandeveer, Price, Elliott and Stidham families. The Delaware Swedish Colonial Society holds an annual and very well attended **Lucia Fest [8]** here every December, near the actual date of the 13th.

Visitor Information

Services Sunday 9:30 a.m.
January & February by appointment only;
March – May: Wednesday – Friday 1:00 p.m. – 4:00 p.m. and Saturday 10:00 a.m. - 4:00 p.m. (morning tours by appointment only); June – December: Wednesday – Saturday: 10:00 a.m. – 4:00 p.m.
Admission: adults $4.00, children (6-12) $2.00, children 5 & under free; grounds free.

Holy Trinity (Old Swedes') Church

606 Church Street, Wilmington, DE 19801
phone: 302-652-5629
email: info@oldswedes.org
web: oldswedes.org

[3]

Hendrickson House

This **ancient stone house [1]**, built about 1690 where the Crum Creek meets the Delaware River in Ridley Township, Pennsylvania, was rescued and rebuilt on the grounds of Holy Trinity in 1959. It was built for Anders Hendrickson, whose grandfather had arrived in 1654 with the last Royal Governor, Johan Rising. It seems to have been a wedding present for Anders and his bride, Birgitta Mårtenson. For almost 120 years it was owned by descendants but then was sold in 1788 and by 1798 doubled in size. Now it serves as the headquarters of the Old Swedes Foundation and the Delaware Swedish Colonial Society. It

includes a museum, archive and bookstore. One of the treasures on permanent display is an **altar antependium [2]** that was hand-crafted by the late King Gustaf V of Sweden in 1950. A superb **silver chalice, paten and host box [3]** sent from the Great Copper Mining Company of Falun, Sweden in 1718 is used on special festival occasions.

Visitor Information

January & February by appointment only;
March – May: Wednesday – Friday 1:00 p.m. – 4:00 p.m.
and Saturday 10:00 a.m. - 4:00 p.m. (morning tours by appointment only); June – December: Wednesday – Saturday: 10:00 a.m. – 4:00 p.m.
Admission: adults $4.00, children (6-12) $2.00, children 5 & under free; grounds free.

Hendrickson House

606 Church Street, Wilmington, DE 19801
phone: 302-652-5629
email: info@oldswedes.org
web: oldswedes.org

[2]

Crane Hook Church Monument & Marker

The congregation was evicted from Ft. Christina after the Dutch conquest in 1655. It was only after the arrival of the English in 1664 that they were given permission to build their first real church building at Crane Hook, a location on the south side of the Christina River. This log church, erected in 1667 with the assistance of Pastor Lars Carlsson Lock, was well-placed to serve the needs of the people at Christina, New Castle and New Jersey, since the primary means of transport was by water. The original location was marked by a stone monument erected by the Historical Society of Delaware in 1896. Unfortunately, this location became heavily industrialized with an oil tank farm and almost no public access. Recent scholarship also doubted that it was in the exact location. In 2012 the New Sweden Centre succeeded in getting a new State of Delaware **Historical marker [4]** and had the original monument moved to a prominent location in **front of the Hendrickson House [5]** (page 26).

This marker [4] was placed by the State of Delaware in 2012 to indicate the approximate site of the Crane Hook Log Church, the predecessor to the stone Holy Trinity Church in Wilmington. It is on the eastern side of Route 9 just north of the Delaware Memorial Bridge. Its wording shows a marked improvement over the previous sign at the same site.

[5]

[4]

Wertmüller House

[1]

Adolf Ulrich Wertmüller (1751-1811) was a gifted Swedish painter who came to America and became a citizen of the new land. He had been an artist at the Royal Courts of France and Sweden and his **portrait of President George Washington [1]**, made while he was President in Philadelphia, is considered one of the finest ever made of the first President. This digital copy of the original at the Philadelphia Museum of Art was made for the Society in 2006. Wertmüller married the granddaughter of Swedish artist Gustavus Hesselius and settled down on a farm in Claymont, Delaware. His home, with its still identifiable picture gallery, is now in deplorable condition and sits in the middle of an abandoned steel mill at the confluence of Naaman's Creek and the Delaware River. The Claymont Historical Society is desperately seeking ways to save it.

Visitor Information

On private property owned by Evraz Claymont Steel.

Wertmüller House

Evraz Claymont Steel
    4001 Philadelphia Pike, Claymont, DE 19703
phone: 302-792-5400
email: info@evrazincna.com
web: claymontsteel.com

New Castle

New Castle is the original capital of Delaware and one of the few remaining colonial landscapes in America, counting 30 public and private buildings of historical stature. It was founded by New Netherland Governor Peter Stuyvesant in 1651 with a fortification known as **Ft. Casimir [1]**. This location effectively made the Swedes' fort across the Delaware River (Elfsborg) obsolete. When the last Governor of New Sweden, Johan Rising, arrived and took over the fort in 1654 he gave the Dutch the

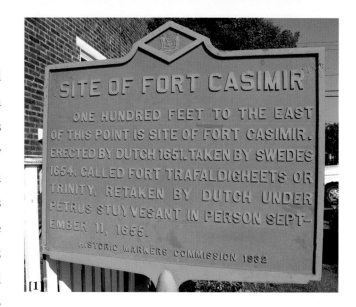

[1]

[2]

excuse they needed to return and with overwhelming force conquer the entire colony (1655). It was renamed New Amstel and the remaining Swedes and Dutch welcomed the English in 1664 when its name became New Castle.

The site of the Dutch and then the Swedish Ft. Trefalighet (Trinity) is marked and the ancient Immanuel Episcopal Church that was founded in 1689 as the first Anglican parish in Delaware with its **massive tower [2]** still dominates the town green. When Immanuel's first church was erected in 1703 the Dedicatory sermon was given by the Swedish pastor at Gloria Dei in Philadelphia, Andreas Rudman, who also named the congregation. Of special interest in the town are also the Court House (1732), the 1700 Dutch House, and the Presbyterian Church (1707) which inherited the members of the Dutch Reformed persuasion.

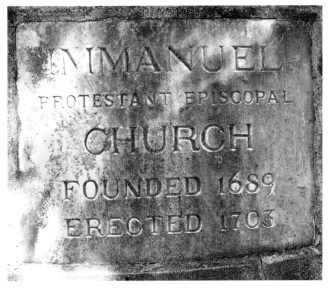

IMMANUEL
PROTESTANT EPISCOPAL
CHURCH
FOUNDED 1689
ERECTED 1703

pennsylvania

Swedish and Finnish immigrants continued to expand beyond Ft. Christina and initially up the west side of the Delaware (South) River, settling first at Upland (Chester) and later at Ammansland (Ridley Township), Calcoon Hook and Kingsessing (West Philadelphia). The many navigable rivers drew them far apart from each other. With the arrival of the third and first royal, Governor Johan Printz in 1643, things began to change. The New Sweden Company was now wholly Swedish, the Swedish investors having bought out the Dutch, and it was now a royal colony. It began to be thought of as more than a trading post. Printz moved the capital from Ft. Christina to the centrally located Tinicum Island (Essington) which he now named New Gothenburg. Here he erected his famed residence, the Printzhof, that was both a gubernatorial mansion and a law court. He also had a church erected that was the first in the Delaware Valley (1646). In this way it could be said that he was the first Governor and Judge in what later became Pennsylvania. His portrait (page 85), courtesy of the Swedish Colonial Society, hangs first in the line of Governors at the Governor's mansion in Harrisburg.

The Swedish cultural hegemony disappeared in 1682 when 23 ships bearing Quakers for Penn's new colony appeared in the River.

Interstate 676

Interstate 76

④

Philadelphia

⑬

⑫

②

④

③

Interstate 76

Interstate 95

New Jersey

① Governor Printz Park

② Gloria Dei (Old Swedes') Church

③ American Swedish Historical Museum

④ City Hall Statue of Swedish Settlers

⑤ Old Swedish Burial Ground

⑥ Monument to Finnish Settlers

⑦ Morton Homestead

⑧ Morton Morton House

⑨ Calcon Hook

⑩ Techoherassi: Olof Stille Site

⑪ Lower Swedish Log Cabin

⑫ St. James Church of Kingsessing

⑬ Bartram's Garden

⑭ Swedes' Mill at Cobbs Creek

⑮ Christ Church Upper Merion

⑯ St. Gabriel's Episcopal Church

⑰ Mouns Jones House

⑱ Brossman Center

Governor Printz Park

The majestic, seven-foot **statue of Governor Johan Printz [1]** was erected by the Swedish Colonial Society in 1972 and created by member Carl Lindborg. It shows the 400-pound Governor overlooking his domain against the background of the Delaware River. The Swedish Colonial Society marked the Tinicum site first with a **granite marker [2]** in 1923 at a site owned by the Corinthian Yacht Club. In 1926 the five acres adjacent to this monument were given to the Society to develop as a park. It took time to clear and grade the property, plant trees

NEW SWEDEN

In 1643 the colony's Governor, Johan Printz, established its capital here on Tinicum Island. Earlier, in 1638, New Sweden had been founded at the site of present Wilmington. Although the colony was captured by the Dutch in 1655, many Swedish and Finnish settlers remained. This was the region's first permanent European settlement, some four decades before William Penn's 1681 founding of Pennsylvania.

PENNSYLVANIA HISTORICAL AND MUSEUM COMMISSION 1969

[1]

[2]

and build a retaining wall but, with the help of the WPA, it began to assume its present appearance. It was deeded to the Commonwealth of Pennsylvania in 1938 as a public park. In 2003 the State deeded it back to Tinicum Township in an economy move but with the provision that it forever be a park. A number of archeological digs have been located here beginning in the 1930's and many artifacts are stored now with the Pennsylvania Historical and Museum Commission in Harrisburg. We know exactly where the Printzhof stood and its size. A number of **yellow Dutch bricks [3]** unearthed at the site were used in the "stuga" of the American Swedish Historical Museum and some are stored in the Society's archives.

Visitor Information

The park is open to the public year round.

Governor Printz Park

Taylor Ave. & Second St., Essington, PA 19029
phone: 610-521-3530
email: info@tinicumtownshipdelco.com
web: cr.nps.gov/history/online_books/explorers/sitec53.htm
    or
    explorepahistory.com/hmarker.php?markerId=34

[3]

Gloria Dei
(Old Swedes') Church

The oldest church in Pennsylvania was built in 1700 by the same construction crews that built Holy Trinity at Christina. It replaced an earlier log building on the same site. It is the same size as Holy Trinity, 60' long, 30' wide and 20' high, but its use of brick and its three-sided apse give it a much more urbane character. The settlers who lived near Tinicum went to that church for a long time but, as people moved northwards, it became inconvenient to use. In 1677 the northern congregation built a blockhouse church at Wicacå and called a Dutch pastor from New York, Jacob Fabritius to be their pastor. At the time Philadelphia did not exist, although today the location is in the southern part of the city near the Delaware River. It is now a part of the Independence National Historical Park and its walled block is an oasis in a gentrifying part of the city known as Queen's Village. Of course, the name refers to Queen Christina who was the monarch during most of the New Sweden Colony's existence. The church is the legal address of the Swedish Colonial Society. The Swedish High Mass continues to be offered here once a month by a Church of Sweden pastor from New York.

The Tinicum building was abandoned but the congregation kept its original Swedish bell and a unique carving showing **angels and an open Bible [1]** with the words from Isaiah on one side, and the angels' song to the shepherds at Christmas on the other. The interior suffered from British troops during the American Revolution and underwent a major renovation in 1846, including the addition of side balconies. None of the furnishings except the

THIS MARBLE COVERS THE
REMAINS
OF THE REVEREND ANDREW RUDMAN:
BEING SENT HITHER FROM SWEDEN,
HE FIRST FOUNDED & BUILT THIS CHURCH.
AS A CONSTANT FAITHFUL PREACHER
IN TH' ENGLISH, SWEDE'S & DUTCH CHURCHES
ELEVEN YEARS IN THIS COUNTREY:
WHERE HE ADVANC'D TRUE PIETY.
BY SOUND DOCTRINE & GOOD EXAMPLE.

HE DIED SEP.R 17 · 1708.
AGED 40 YEARS.

[3]

1732 marble font can claim to be close to the originals. Although the windows have been enlarged they retain the plain glass of the originals, except for a nondescript colored glass widow in the chancel. A sad note is seen in the **double gravestone [2]** which marks the graves of two infant sons of Pastor Andreas Sandel.

The **grave stone [3]** at the head of the center aisle marks the short life of Andreas Rudman, who came in 1697 with the first group of three priests to renew the mission of the Church of Sweden in America and led the work to build the current structure in 1700. He gave the church its unusual name. The Latin Gloria Dei means "The Glory of God." The hanging ship models of the **Kalmar Nyckel [4]** and the *Fogel Grip* along with the brass chandelier were given by Carl Milles in 1938. Nicholas (Nils) Collin was the last Swedish pastor on the Delaware and served here until his death in 1831. His successor, Jehu Curtis Clay wrote the first history of New Sweden in English, *The Annals of the Swedes on the Delaware.*

[5]

[2]

[4]

[1]

Both Jenny Lind and Fredrika Bremer visited the congregation. The present **organ [1]** is a fine Hook and Hastings that was installed in 1903 and restored in 1993. Since the time that Andreas Rudman had two small hymnals printed in 1700 the congregation has been known for its fine music. The angel **Gabriel [5]**, hanging in the chancel, is a 20th century replica of such a Swedish angel as seen in parishes in western Sweden; the angel Gabriel ready to sound the trumpet for the Final Day when "God's Glory" will be known over all the earth.

Visitor Information

Services Sunday 10:00 a.m.

Gloria Dei (Old Swedes') Church

916 S. Swanson St. (Columbus Blvd. & Christian St.)
    Philadelphia, PA 19147
phone: 215-389-1513
email: info@old-swedes.org
web: old-swedes.org

American Swedish Historical Museum

The Swedish museum was built between 1926 and 1938 in League Island, later Franklin Delano Roosevelt Park, in South Philadelphia. Its bucolic setting and grand design were inspired by Swedish manors of the 17th century. It was the first Swedish Museum in this country and its prime mover was Amandus Johnson, one of the founders of the Swedish Colonial Society. It is dedicated to **John Morton [1]**, who was one of those from Pennsylvania, and the only Scandinavian, who signed the Declaration of Independence in 1776.

Visitor Information

Tuesday to Friday: 10:00 a.m. to 4:00 p.m.;
Saturday & Sunday, noon to 4:00 p.m.

American Swedish Historical Museum

1900 Pattison Ave., Philadelphia, PA 19145
phone: 215-389-1776
email: info@americanswedish.org
web: americanswedish.org

Philadelphia
City Hall Statues

At the very center of Philadelphia, William Penn planned a park on the central square. This square is now the location of the fabulous French Renaissance City Hall, with its huge stature of William Penn looking northeast towards the location of the site of his treaty with the local Lenape. On the next level, below Penn, are these two representations of colonial Swedish settlers, looking south and east towards the Swedish settlement of Wicacå and Gloria Dei (Old Swedes') Church. All of the statuary was completed by Alexander Milne Calder (grandfather of the famed mobile artist) who worked on hundreds of sculptures during the 30 years it took to complete the huge structure. At the southern entry on Broad Street is a plaque dedicated in 1909, the same year that the Swedish Colonial Society was formed. This plaque, funded by the Society of Colonial Dames, memorializes the New Sweden Colony by giving a description of its geography and listing its governors and 10 prominent families.

Visitor Information

The City Hall Tower Observation Deck is open Monday to Friday, 9:30 a.m. to noon for school group tours & noon to 4:15 p.m. for general admission. For tours and tower admission, visit the Tour Information Center in Room 121.

City Hall Statues of Swedish Settlers

Broad St. & Market St., Philadelphia, PA 19107
phone: 215-686-2840
web: freepages.genealogy.rootsweb.ancestry.com/
    ~wjohn55447/City%20Hall.htm
    or
    phila.gov/virtualch

Old Swedish Burial Ground

The glebe for the church at Tinicum was not on that island but on the mainland near what is now Chester Creek. The first pastor of this new church was Johan Campanius (1643-1648) who then named the glebe area for his home province, Uppland. Here he wrote the first draft of his famous version of Martin Luther's "Small Catechism" – the very first book ever printed in the Algonquin language. The land was later the site of the first building of St. Paul's Church (1702) that served the many Swedes and English people that found it difficult to travel to Philadelphia. Among those who attended St. Paul's as well as Gloria Dei, and later contributed to building of St. James in Kingsessing, was the Pennsylvania politician and surveyor John Morton (1725-1777). He was descended from Mårten Mårtenson who came to America in 1654 from "Finland in Sweden" as was noted in the Gloria Dei church book. John Morton was sheriff in Chester County before being elected to the Provincial Assembly, as both delegate and then Speaker and then finally to the First Continental Congress where he signed the Declaration of Independence. Upland was also the site of the "Upland Court," the Swedish judicial body that ruled from 1656-1680 when first the Dutch, and then the English, gave the Swedes semi-autonomy as the "Swedish Nation" or "Upland County."

Visitor Information

The cemetery is open to the public year round.

Old Swedish Burial Ground
Third St. & Market St. (Ave. of the States),
    Chester PA 19013
phone: 610-872-0502
email: dchs.pa@gmail.com
web: oldchesterpa.com/cemeteries/
    stpcemetery.htm

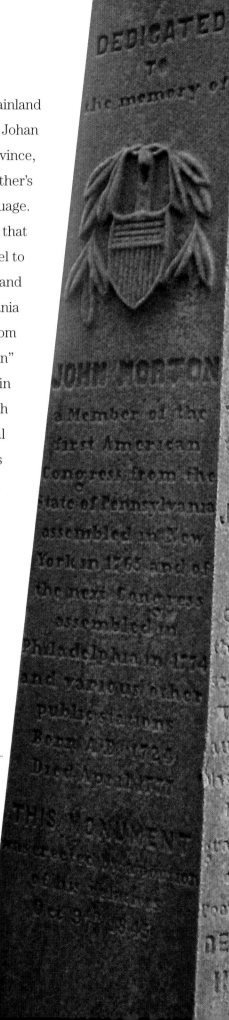

Monument to Finnish Settlers

Part of Upland (Chester) was known as Finland because of the many Finns who settled there, especially under Dutch and English rule. In 1938 this beautiful red-brown Balmoral granite monument was carved by noted Finnish sculptor Vaino Aaltonen. It was dedicated on June 29, just after the Swedish monument at the Rocks in Wilmington, to celebrate the Tercentenary of New Sweden. The stone was quarried in Finland and sits on a black base from Rautalampi. It was moved to its present location near Kerlin Street from Crozer Park in 1955 because of the construction of I-95.

Visitor Information

The monument is open to the public year round.

Monument to Finnish Settlers
1145 Concord Ave., Chester PA 19013
phone: 610-872-0502
email: dchs.pa@gmail.com
web: explorepahistory.com/hmarker.
    php?markerId=33

Morton Homestead

This ancient log house on the Darby Creek, north of Tinicum, is composed of three separate sections – the two older log sections and the stone part that joins them. The north section was built by Matthias Mårtenson, son of the original immigrant, in the 1690s. The south section was built about 1760 over the remains of the original Mårtenson log home. At one time it was thought that John Morton was born here but there is no evidence to support that. Just now the ancient home is endangered since the Pennsylvania Historical and Museum Commission has decided to "de-accession" it due to severe budget restraints imposed by the legislature. Indeed, the record of the Commonwealth in maintaining this site is poor and includes taking it entirely apart and rebuilding it after soaking the logs with creosote, turning the wood black. It is unfurnished and has now been given officially to the Borough of Prospect Park.

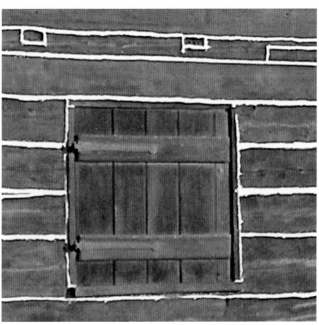

Visitor Information

The homestead is presently closed to the public.
For access, contact Borough of Prospect Park.

Morton Homestead

100 Lincoln Ave. (Rte. 420), Prospect Park, PA 19076
phone: 610-532-1007
web: prospectparkboro.com

Morton Morton House

Located just up the Creek from the older Morton Homestead, at the confluence of the Darby and Muckinipattus Creeks, this fine English style brick home was built by Morton Morton in ca. 1750, a great grandson of the original settler and a first cousin of the Signer, John Morton. It remained in the family until 1873 and was later abandoned. It is now owned by the Borough of Norwood and maintained by the Norwood Historical Society. Restoration of the exterior was completed in 2005 and work on the interior is on-going.

Visitor Information

June to September: Sunday 1:00 p.m. to 4:00 p.m. Additional tours can be arranged by calling the Norwood Borough office 610-586-5800.

Morton Morton House

517 E. Winona Ave., Norwood, PA 19074
phone: 610-586-5800
web: norwoodpahistorical.org

Calcon Hook

Calcon Hook or Turkey Point was the next Swedish settlement up Mill Creek above Amosland but below Kingsessing. Israel Acrelius related that it was named for "the wild turkeys that harboured there in great numbers." *Kalkon* in Swedish means turkey. The area was located behind Tinicum Island. Calcon Hook was home to the families of Petersson/Stake, Urian, Mortonsson and Boon. Later, Swedish descendants had hopes of another church being built there, however that did not happen. Today, the settlement is within the bounds of the Boroughs of Folcroft, Glenolden and Sharon Hill.

Techoherassi: Olof Stille Site

Above the winding Ridley Creek (Olof Stilles kil) is the site where Olof Stille settled in 1641. The ancient additions to the imposing brick home of Joseph Sharpless (1700 & 1750) may be on the second site since it has Swedish building details and has been dated to 1685. A **rock near the creek with the date 1682 [1]** identifies what is thought to be the original site nearer the water. The initials IS probably mean John Sharples, the first Sharples in America, but it could also indicate the last Swede to own the site, John Stille, Olof's son. The home is in the middle of a 20th century housing development and is not open to the public. Interestingly enough, his English neighbors called him Wolley Stille and the main house retains this name.

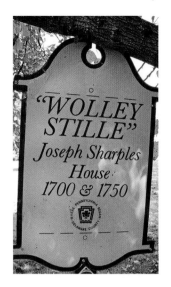

"WOLLEY STILLE" Joseph Sharples House 1700 & 1750

[1]

Visitor Information

The home is privately owned and not open to the public.

Techoherassi: Olof Stille Site

Harvey Road & Maple Road,
Nether Providence Township, PA 19086
web: delcohistory.org/nphs

Lower Swedish Log Cabin

This difficult-to-locate ancient log house has typical Swedish/Finnish details, including stone corner fireplaces and V-notching. It seems to date from 1697. It is located in Upper Darby Township near Drexel Hill in a deep valley of the Darby Creek that shuts out the surrounding row houses. It is indeed a fine colonial location and seems like a dream from the 17th century. It was restored and furnished by The "Friends of the Swedish Log Cabin" in 1989. The former Upper Log Cabin was severely harmed by fire and dismantled in 1980.

Visitor Information

The cabin is closed to the public. Group tours may be arranged in advance by calling 610-237-8064.

Lower Swedish Log Cabin

9 Creek Rd. (Box 200), Drexel Hill, PA 19026
phone: 610-237-8064
email: theswedishcabin@comcast.net
web: swedishcabin.org

St. James Church of Kingsessing

This congregation was founded by Pastor Carl Magnus Wrangel who was pastor at Gloria Dei from 1759-1768. It was one of the "Annex" congregations that were united with Gloria Dei and served by their pastors and a joint Vestry until 1841. The original stone building was erected in 1762, with most of the stone masonry being done by members of the congregation. The building was significantly enlarged with transepts and a chancel in 1859. The church and its large graveyard with parish house and rectory take up a whole city block in what is now a struggling area of Southwest Philadelphia. In 1962, at its 300th anniversary, the Swedish Colonial Society presented the congregation with a Swedish granite **cornerstone [1]** to replace the one that had been lost in the 1859 construction.

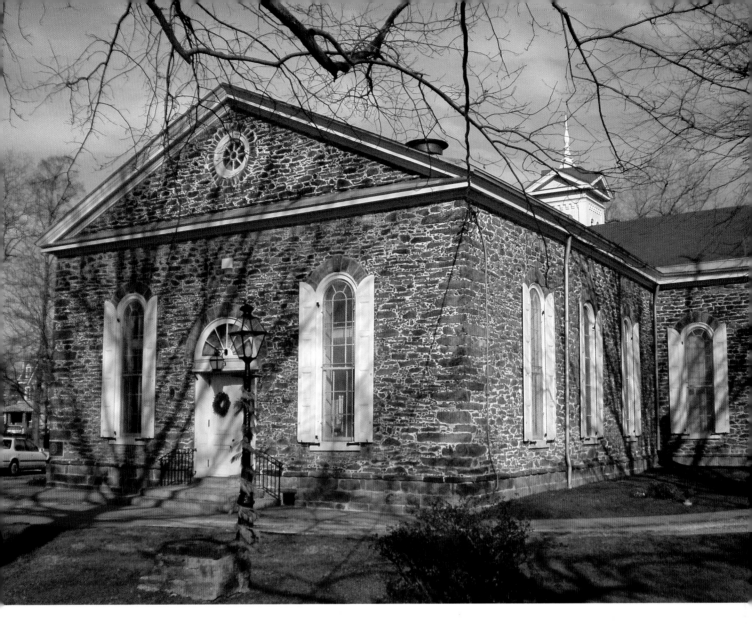

[1]

Visitor Information

Services Sunday 8:15 a.m. & 10:30 a.m.

St. James Church of Kingsessing

6838 Woodland Ave., Philadelphia, PA 19142
phone: 215-727-5265
email: stjameskingsessing@gmail.com
web: stjameschurchofkingsessing.com

Bartram's Garden

This historic site that once was a Swedish plantation (Måns Jonasson) is now the restored home of John and William Bartram, Quaker botanists who were friends with many of the Swedish pastors in the Delaware Valley and especially Pehr Kalm, the disciple of Carl Linnaeus who traveled around the area between 1748-1751. The state flower of Pennsylvania, the Mountain Laurel (*Kalmia Multiflora*), is named for him. In 2007 during the 300th anniversary of the birth of Linnaeus, various places in the world were designated as UNESCO World Heritage Linnean sites showing that one of the Linnean disciples had been there and exchanged plants and ideas. Bartram's Gardens holds such a designation and has contacts with the Royal Agricultural University in Sweden. Two historic Rambo apple trees were planted here in 2009.

Visitor Information

The grounds are free and open to the public year round, except on Philadelphia city-observed holidays. Group tours are available year round with advance registration. General admission tours of both the house & historic garden are available on weekends only from May through October.

Bartram's Garden

54th St. & Lindbergh Blvd., Philadelphia, PA 19143
phone: 215-729-1047
email: info@bartramsgarden.org
web: bartramsgarden.org

Where Pennsylvania History Began
by Henry D. Paxson (Swedish Colonial Society 1926)

[1]

Printz's (Old Swedes') Mill at Cobbs Creek

It was known as Mölndahl by the Swedes or "Mill Valley" and could be considered the site of the first manufacturing in the Delaware Valley. On the western border of the city of Philadelphia above Baltimore Avenue, the site is still visible where Governor Johan Printz established a grist mill in 1646. In 1926 the Swedish Colonial Society and the Colonial Dames of America erected a **replica Norse mill [1]** at the site with the assistance of the Nordic Museum in Stockholm. Two years later a hurricane wiped away every trace of the replica mill.

Visitor Information

The site is open to the public year round. The mill structure no longer exists but the square anchoring holes remain visible below the mill dam (constructed later).

Printz's (Old Swedes') Mill at Cobbs Creek

Woodland Ave. & Island Ave., Philadelphia, PA 19142
phone: 610-583-4386
web: hmdb.org/marker.asp?marker=28207
    or
    darbyhistory.com/SwedesMill.html

Christ Church Upper Merion

This is the other country annex that Gloria Dei founded, in 1763, although pastors had services in homes and a school house since 1735. The original nave was extended with transepts, tower and a chancel in 1837. Further renovatons led to Gothic windows in 1865 and in 1883 the tower was redesigned and raised 20 feet. The red granite baptismal font, carved in Västervik, was a gift from friends in Sweden in 1885 and has the inscription: "Sweden's blessings to Sweden's children." The outstanding collection of **stained glass windows** created by pioneer artist, Paula Himmelsbach Belano (1877-1967), show the history of New Sweden and the history of salvation in a brilliant and exciting way. The windows were installed between 1938 and 1948. They are a priceless artistic treasure. The congregation also owns a unique "Union" flag presented by Prince Oscar in 1876. This was the last of the eight Old Swedes' churches to join the Episcopal Church, finally taking the legal steps in 1957. It is now a very small congregation. Its large and fascinating cemetery contains many Swedish names, including Rambo, Holstein and Yocum. It is in the neighborhood of Swedesburg in the town of Bridgeport on the west side of the Schuylkill, adjacent to I-276, the Pennsylvania Turnpike.

Visitor Information

Services Sunday 10:00 a.m.

Christ Church Upper Merion

740 River Rd., Swedesburg, PA 19405
phone: 610-272-6036 or 610-283-5769
email: oldswedes@gmail.com
web: facebook.com/pages/Christ-Church-Old-Swedes-
    Swedesburg-PA/328590651735?v=wall

Saint James 1762

N Collin D.D.
1746 1831

1700 AD
Gloria Dei

Christ Church
Lower Merion

The Voyage of the
Swan
1638

Catechismvs Lutheri

First Church
Tinicum Island
1646
The

Hell

Johan Campanius
1643-1648

St. Gabriel's Episcopal Church

This congregation in Amity Township at Douglassville in Berks County began as a district of Gloria Dei church which the pastors visited regularly because of the settlement of Swedes in nearby Manatawny. Upon the intercession of Pastor Andreas Rudman with William Penn, land further up the Schuylkill was given to the Swedes in exchange for being cheated of so much property in Philadelphia. The first log church was erected in 1736 and was named for the former pastor of Gloria Dei, Gabriel Falk, who was serving the congregation before returning to Sweden. The 1801 **red fieldstone building [1]** after having been used for educational purposes for 70 years was restored from 1960-1975. The oldest legible **cemetery stone [2]** is that of Andrew Robeson (1719), a Justice of the Peace under William Penn with a Swedish wife that he had met in New Jersey, Maria Helm. Since the congregation was so far inland, it was difficult to have regular services so that in 1762 the congregation joined the Anglican mission in Reading in calling a priest from England to serve both congregations. It was thus the first of the Pennsylvania Swedish churches to call a pastor from the Anglican Communion – a pattern which all the other seven Old Swedes churches would also follow. The large Gothic stone church on the other side of the cemetery was built in 1887.

[2]

Visitor Information

Services Saturday 6:00 p.m.; Sunday 8:00 a.m. & 10:30 a.m.

St. Gabriel's Episcopal Church

1188 Ben Franklin Hwy. E. (Rte. 422),
    Douglassville, PA 19518
phone: 610-385-3144
email: office@stgabriels.us
web: stgabriels.us

Mouns Jones House

Nearby is the Mouns Jones (Måns Jonasson) house in Old Morlatton Village. It is the oldest structure in Berks County. It has corner fireplaces, a beehive oven and a date stone showing 1716. Here in Old Morlatton Village a fall Mouns Jones Festival is an annual fair.

Visitor Information

The House is open only during special events or by reservation 610-385-4762.

Mouns Jones House

Old Philadelphia Pike, Douglassville, PA 19518
phone: 610-385-4762
email: info@historicpreservationtrust.org
web: historicpreservationtrust.org/historic-
properties/morlatton-village/mouns-jones-house

Brossman Center

The major classroom building at the Lutheran Theological Seminary in the Mt. Airy section of Philadelphia, it was constructed in 2004 and is the home of the Lutheran Archives Center, as well as the Archives of the Swedish Colonial Society comprising the institutional records, the Craig Collection, and the Rambo Collection. The Brossman Center also houses the Augustana Institute and Museum, which are devoted to displaying and preserving resources related to the 19th and early 20th century Swedish immigration to the northeast. The **Rambo apple tree [1]** in the foreground is one of the many historical trees that were planted in Sweden and America through the Rambo Apple Friendship Project. Peter Gunnarson Rambo brought the first Rambo apples to the Delaware Valley in 1640. This apple variety unfortunately died out in Sweden in 1708 but was recently re-introduced. It serves as a reminder of the New Sweden colony in places as diverse as the Haga Royal Palace in Sweden, the Swedish Museum in Philadelphia and in Lindsborg, Kansas.

Visitor Information

The Brossman Center is on the grounds of The Lutheran Theological Seminary at Philadelphia.

Brossman Center

7301 Germantown Avenue, Philadelphia, PA 19119
phone: 215-248-7339 or 866.548.7339
web: brossmancenter.com

[1]

1. Fort Elfsborg
2. Trinity Episcopal (Old Swedes') Church & Schorn Log Cabin
3. Mullica House
4. Moravian Church Oldman's Creek
5. C.A. Nothnagle Log House
6. St. George's Episcopal (Old Swedes') Church
7. New Sweden Heritage Monument
8. Johan Printz Park Log Cabin
9. Tyler (Hancock) Log House
10. New Sweden Colonial Farmstead Museum & Living History Center
11. Swedish Granary
12. Caesar Hoskins Log Cabin
13. Moravian Church Maurice River
14. Steelman (Stille) Family Cemetery

new jersey

The soil appeared better on the west side of the Delaware River, hence the Swedish and Finnish settlements on the east side were later and began around 1671 with Finn's Point near Pennsville and then New Stockholm, Repaupo, Great Mantua Creek and finally all the way north to Senamensing (Cinnaminson). There were English settlers from New Haven near Salem on Varkens Kill during the time of Govenor Printz, but the Governor deemed them not a threat to his jurisdiction or trade. After the English replaced the Dutch in 1664, the area was named New Jersey and was given to two friends of King James II, Sir George Carteret and Lord Berkeley. Because of difficulties in collecting taxes, Lord Berkeley sold his West Jersey half of the colony to the Quakers in 1673. John Fenwick then settled his colony in Salem (1675) before Penn had arrived on the scene. The rural Swedish settlers who were all in the West Jersey area continued to thrive under English rule and even after the colony was reunited as one Royal colony in 1702.

Fort Elfsborg

When Governor Printz arrived in 1643 he realized that the military defenses of the colony needed immediate improvement. He chose a place near the mouth of the Salem River for a fortification which he named after the famous Elvsborg in Gothenburg harbor. The community nearby is known today as Elsinboro. It was a perfect spot from which to guard and control the traffic on the River. At this location sandbars force all shipping to hug the eastern coast. It also had the advantage of being a place from which the nearby English could be observed. It is reported to have been constructed of earthen works, had three angles, was manned by 17 soldiers and had eight cannons and one mortar. By 1651 it was abandoned because the Dutch had erected Ft. Casimir (later called New Castle) in an even more advantageous location on the west bank. The exact location of Ft. Elfsborg has never been adequately ascertained. Some think that it is now covered by water. Others suggest that Printz left behind canons that are buried in the area. Since most of this area now belongs to the Salem Nuclear Generating Station, access is severely limited. Legends about the mosquitoes in the area seem exaggerated.

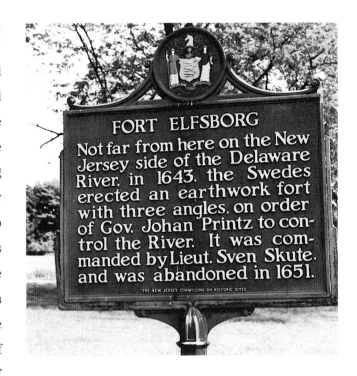

FORT ELFSBORG
Not far from here on the New Jersey side of the Delaware River, in 1643, the Swedes erected an earthwork fort with three angles, on order of Gov. Johan Printz to control the River. It was commanded by Lieut. Sven Skute, and was abandoned in 1651.

THE NEW JERSEY COMMISSION ON HISTORIC SITES

Visitor Information

The exact location of the fort is unknown and, therefore, may be on public land, on private property, or under water.

Fort Elfsborg

It is generally thought that the fort is located south of Elsinboro, NJ, perhaps near the mouth of Mill Creek.

web: http://en.wikipedia.org/wiki/Fort_Nya_Elfsborg

Trinity Episcopal (Old Swedes') Church

In Sveaborg (Swedesboro) a congregation was organized as early as 1703. The name of the area was originally Raccoon but the new name honors the mighty fortress in the Helsinki Harbor. At first the settlers in New Jersey attended either Holy Trinity at Christina or Gloria Dei in Philadelphia. Yet the distance was long and foul weather often prevented them from reaching their goal. The first pastor, Lars Tollstadius arrived without the permission of Bishop Jesper Svedberg who was in charge of the pastoral needs of the churches from 1697 until his death in 1735. Both Pennsylvania pastors opposed the new congregation because they had pledges and debts on their new church buildings. In spite of opposition, a log church was dedicated in 1705 and 100 acres of land were purchased for a glebe. In 1715 the parish was

finally officially recognized in Sweden and a pastor called to serve both Sveaborg and the settlers in Penn's Neck (Pennsville). Considerable troubles ensued from Moravian missionaries who drew some of the members away into a congregation at Oldman's Creek in 1743. The Moravians also built a chapel on the Maurice River (Port Elizabeth) but were unable to regularly staff it for Swedes who had moved south (1746). Special mention should be made of the naturalist Pehr Kalm who visited Sveaborg from 1748-49 and, after the death of the Pastor Johan Sandin, married his widow, served as Lay reader for a year and then moved back to

[2]

[4]

[3]

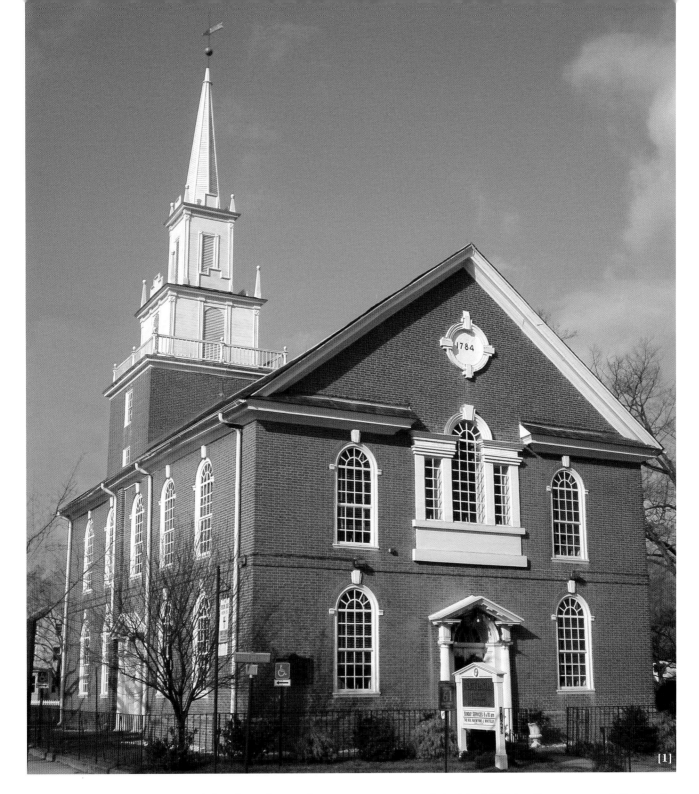

[1]

Finland where he was ordained and taught at the University of Åbo (Turku). Nils Collin served the congregation during the Revolution and led the congregation in building the present impressive **brick church [1]** (1783-1786). It is the largest of the Old Swedes eight churches being 61' by 41' with a **balcony [2]** around three sides. Note the builders' initials on the bricks and a message in Latin from the pastor. The beautiful Georgian tower and steeple were completed in 1839 by the same architect who built the tower of Independence Hall in Philadelphia. The parish owns a marvelous silver Communion **chalice [3]** and **paten [4]** from the early 18th century. The roof and steeple were restored and strengthened in 1996. The **large cemetery [5]** includes a memorial to Eric Mullica. A small park honoring Crown Princess Victoria is across the street.

Schorn Log Cabin

An area north of the **cemetery [5]** where the first log church stood high above the Raccoon Creek was dedicated as the New Sweden Park in 1976. In 1984 the Lear/Mårtenson Log Cabin was received from the Schorn family farm by the Gloucester County Historical Society and located here. It came from the Grand Sprute Plantation on the Raccoon Creek, owned by descendants of Mårten Mårtenson. Since it has no windows it appears to have been a store house or smokehouse of some sort.

Visitor Information

Services: Sunday 8:00 a.m. & 10:00 a.m.

Trinity Episcopal (Old Swedes') Church

1129 Kings Highway (Kings Highway & Church Street)
    P.O. Box 31
    Swedesboro, NJ 08085
phone: 856-467-1227
email: trinityoldswedes@comcast.net
web: trinityswedesboro.org

Mullica House

This may be the only colonial site that has come to light with a Finnish connection. Its seems to have been built in 1704 by one or more of the sons of immigrant Eric Pålsson Mullica, who arrived in New Sweden in 1654. His sons, William, John and Eric moved here five miles up the Raccoon Creek from Swedesboro. The right side portion is the oldest and is of brick-panel frame construction, resting on a stone foundation. One long main support beam supports the length of the original portion of the house. Extensive renovations and additions have not left any corner fireplaces but further investigation will no doubt substantiate its age. It is located on busy State Route 45 in Mullica Hill, Harrison Township in Gloucester County, NJ.

Visitor Information

The house is privately owned and not open to the public.

Mullica House

20 N. Main St., Mullica Hill, NJ 08062
web: colonialswedes.org/Forefathers/Mullica

C.A. Nothnagle Log House

This late 17th century home is attached to a house which, since 1907, has been owned by members of the Nothnagel family. It is near Paulsboro and the site was owned by Andrew Robeson. It has only one room, a corner fireplace and the wood is oak. It could have been built by Israel Helm or by Benjamin Braman following Swedish building methods.

Visitor Information

The cabin is open by appointment only through the current owners who reside in the adjoining structure.

C.A. Nothnagle Log House

406 Swedesboro Rd., Gibbstown, NJ 08027
web: wikipedia.org/wiki/C._A._Nothnagle_Log_House

St. George's Episcopal (Old Swedes') Church

This congregation was named for George I, the King of England and the patron of England, at an area known as Penn's Neck and today as Pennsville. It was organized in 1714 and became part of the Sveaborg/Swedesboro pastoral charge. The first log church was dedicated on the present site in 1717 and enlarged in 1766. The present brick building was constructed in 1808 and extensively renovated with a Gothic spire and windows in 1877. The site is a few blocks from the original ferry landing that connected Finn's Pont with Christina, Delaware.

The congregation has its own **bridal crown [1]** for women married here, an old tradition in Sweden and in Swedish background congregations that refers to the Virgin Mary. It was given by a group of Swedish visitors in 1964 during the 250th anniversary of the congregation. The Parish house dates from 1953.

[1]

Image inspired by a prize–winning photo by Robert M. Harris.

Visitor Information

Services: Sunday 7:30 a.m. & 10:00 a.m.

St. George's Episcopal (Old Swedes') Church

3 Church Landing Road (305 North Broadway),
    Pennsville, NJ 08070
phone: 856-678-7979
email: parish@stgeorgeschurch.us
web: webspace.webring.com/people/ip/pennsville

New Sweden Heritage Monument

Erected in 2004, the newest monument to the native people and colonial ancestors is located in Riverview Beach Park, a picturesque community park on Route 49 that has a fine view of the twin spans of the Delaware Memorial Bridge. The natural, five-ton, five-foot, serpentinite obelisk contains two bronze plaques: "The Delaware River – Colonial Highway of the Swedes and Finns" on the face, and "Land of the Lenape – Settlement of the Swedes and Finns" on the reverse.

Visitor Information

The monument is open to the public year round.

New Sweden Heritage Monument
West Pittsfield St. at the Delaware River,
    Pennsville, NJ 08070
web: swedishheritage.us/2004_monument.php

Johan Printz Park Log Cabin

Built by master carpenter Gunnar Zetterquist for the town of Salem in honor of the 350th anniversary of New Sweden in 1988. It shows one of the earliest types of log structures that were constructed in the colony with a dirt floor, corner chimney and a shake roof.

Visitor Information

The park is open to the public year round. The log cabin is open for special events and reenactments.

John Printz Park Log Cagin

Market St. at the Fenwick Creek Bridge, Salem, NJ 08079
web: http://www.visitsalemcountynj.com/default.asp?
        contentID=14

Tyler (Hancock) Log House

It is notable for its white, hand-hewn, long cedar planks. It originally stood on the property of John Tyler in Salem and was rebuilt on this site in 1934 by the Civil Works Administration. While it does show Swedish building techniques, the interior is furnished with rescued woodwork from other nearby 18th century homes in Salem County. Owned by the State of New Jersey, it stands on the property of the William and Sarah Hancock House (1734). This splendid English Quaker brick mansion is the site of a massacre of colonial militiamen in 1778 by 300 British soldiers.

Visitor Information

Tyler (Hancock) Log House

3 Front St., Hancock's Bridge, NJ 08038
phone: 856-935-4373
email: hancockhousenj@comcast.net
web: http://www.state.nj.us/dep/parksandforests/
    historic/hancockhouse/hancockhouse-swed-
    cabin.htm

New Sweden Colonial Farmstead Museum & Living History Center

In City Park off Commerce Street in the city of Bridgeton. This reconstruction was designed and built by master builder Gunnar Zetterquist from Dala-Floda, Sweden for the 1988 celebrations. The village consists of seven furnished buildings. It has been largely neglected since its opening due to low community support and the lack of other New Sweden sites in the immediate area. Currently, a group of concerned citizens is cataloging the artifacts, many of which came from Sweden, and consulting about future alternatives. Open only by appointment.

Visitor Information

The museum is open during festivals, fairs, reenactments and other public events

New Sweden Colonial Farmstead Museum & Living History Center

Bridgeton City Park
    Mayor Aiken Drive
    31 West Commerce Street
    Bridgeton, New Jersey 08302
web: newswedenfarmstead.org

Swedish Granary

Moved to its present site in the historic area of Greenwich in 1988. Some of the logs are 30 feet in length and are laid without chinking of any kind. It is owned by the Cumberland County Historical Society.

Visitor Information

The granary is located on the grounds of the Cumberland County Historical Society, which is open Tuesday thru Saturday, 1:00 p.m. to 4:00 p.m., but closed January, February & March.

Swedish Granary

Cumberland County Historical Society
> Gibbon House Museum
> Ye Greate Street
> PO Box 16
> Greenwich, New Jersey 08323

phone: 856-455-4055

email: cchistsoc@verizon.net

web: cchistsoc.org

Moravian Church on Oldman's Creek

The Swedish Lutheran pastor Daniel Paul Bryzelius, who for a time was a Moravian missionary in New Jersey, led some members of the Swedesboro and Penn's Neck congregations out of their original churches and dedicated a log church on Oldman's Creek in 1747. The log building was replaced by the present brick structure that was later turned over, ironically enough, to the Episcopal Diocese of New Jersey. For many years there has not been a congregation and it is rarely open. It is a reminder of a painful history of pastoral vacancies, religious rivalry and competition. The map from the Moravian Historical Society is thought to have helped itinerant Moravian missionaries.

Visitor Information

This church property is owned by the Gloucester County Historical Society, Woodbury, NJ.

Moravian Church on Oldman's Creek
King's Highway & Moravian Church Road,
    Swedesboro, NJ 08085
phone: 856-845-4771
email: gchs@net-gate.com
web: nj.searchroots.com/Gloucesterco/moravian.html

Moravian Church Site on Maurice River

Visitor Information

The site is on private property.

Moravian Church Site on Maurice River

Spring Garden Road at Maurice River
    Port Elizabeth, NJ 08348
web: http://www.co.cumberland.nj.us/content
    /163/235/994/1145.aspx

Only this doorstep remains from a log church and cemetery dedicated 36 miles southwest of Pennsville. Swedish settlers who moved south from Swedesboro and Penns Neck made up the congregation that the Moravian missionaries served when they dedicated a church here in 1745. Established by Moravians, it was later served by Swedish pastors who occasionally rode south from Swedesboro-Pennsville. The doorstep is on private property near the Maurice River.

Caesar Hoskins Log Cabin

The Maurice River, a southern tributary of the Delaware, attracted settlers from Swedesboro by the middle of the 18th century. In Cumberland County at an area now called Port Elizabeth, it was not destined to grow, although this Caesar Hoskins Log House shows its Swedish-Finnish construction. The Moravian built chapel in 1745 was soon deserted and the remaining population were absorbed later by the Methodist church. This represents the southernmost settlement of a group of Swedes and Finns.

Visitor Information

The log cabin is open to the public by appointment only.

Caesar Hoskins Log Cabin
Corner of South & Second Streets, Mauricetown, NJ 08329
email: history@mauricetownhistoricalsociety.org
web: www.co.cumberland.nj.us/
content/163/235/851/1067.aspx

Steelman (Stille) Family Cemetery

At Great Egg Harbor near Atlantic City was another Swedish settlement that represented settlers moving east from Swedesboro. It is now known only by this Steelman (Stille) family grave yard. Both Maurice River and Egg Harbor were visited by pastors from Swedesboro, as well as Salem and Friesburg.

Visitor Information

The cemetery is in Estell Manor Park, which is open 7:30 a.m. to dusk.

Steelman (Stille) Family Cemetery
Estell Manor Park

109 State Highway 50, Mays Landing, NJ 08330
phone: 856-645-5960
web: findagrave.com/cgi-bin/
    fg.cgi?page=cr&CRid=2156688

Interstate 95

John F. Kennedy
Memorial Highway

Maryland

Elkton

West Pulaski Highway

1 North East

2

Augustine
Herman
Highway

Turkey
Point
Road

Mexico Ave NW

5

Connecticut Ave NW

Massachusetts Ave NW

Wisconsin Ave NW

Chesapeake City

Rock Creek & Potomac Pkwy NW

Reservoir Rd NW

Washington, DC

3

Route 310
(Cayot's Corner Rd.)

Canal Rd NW

M St NW

Potomac River

4 K St NW

1 St. Mary Anne's Episcopal Church

4 Embassy of Sweden

2 John Hans Steelman House at
Historic Elk Landing

5 Embassy of Finland

3 Coon's Log Cabin

maryland and washington, d.c.

Swedish and Finnish settlers drifted west on the Delmarva Peninsula beginning with the harsh rule of Governor Johan Printz, although not in as great numbers as in Pennsylvania and New Jersey. The colony had been granted to the Calvert family in 1632 and the first settlers arrived at St. Mary's, on the southern West Shore, in 1634. Annapolis as a new capital for the colony was not laid out until 1694.

The uncertain boundary lines between Pennsylvania, Maryland and Delaware were not finally settled until 1767 with the famous Mason-Dixon survey. The rich alluvial lands of the Eastern Shore and the water transport across the Christina River to the Head of Elk made communications fairly easy. This was, of course, one of the reasons that Peter Minuit wanted to begin New Sweden at the Rocks.

St. Mary Anne's Episcopal Church

So many Swedes had moved west of Wilmington (Christina) that Elkton was know as "Swedes Town" and thus a church was organized by 1702 by Jonas Aurén, one of the three priests who arrived in 1697 to revive the mission of the Church of Sweden on the Delaware. It was called St. Mary's and the town is now North East.

After four years of work, land beside the river was purchased and the first log building was erected. After Aurén's death and a long pastoral vacancy, an Anglican priest was called (1722) since the Anglican Church was by then established in Maryland. The present **brick building [1]** was erected after the first church burned in 1743. The name was changed to reflect the

[1]

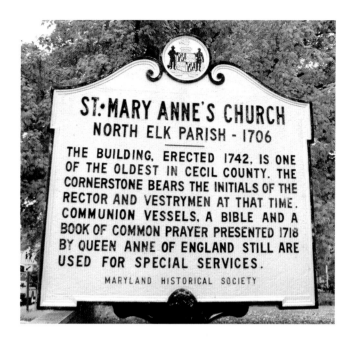

gratitude of the congregation for the gifts from Queen Anne's estate of a large Bible, Book of Common Prayer and silver Communion ware. The tower was added in 1904 and the Vestry House in 1970.

When the Virginia style Vestry house was erected a number of **Indian graves [2]** were discovered and authenticated by the Smithsonian Institution. We know that Aurén made a number of missionary journeys among the Conestoga Indians and that he used the newly printed Catechism that he had with him and that had been translated by Johan Campanius in 1648. Since it was the European custom to allow only baptized persons to be buried in a church cemetery, e.g. consecrated ground, and since Lenape custom was to bury alone in the forests, this must be taken as an example of successful Indian conversions to Christianity. It is a reminder of the famed good relationship between New Sweden, the Lenape and the Minquas.

Visitor Information

Services: Sunday 8:00 a.m. & 10:30 a.m., and
Wednesday 10:30 a.m.

St. Mary Anne's Episcopal Church

315 South Main Street
    North East, MD 21901
phone: 410-287-5522
email: office@stmaryanne.org
web: stmaryanne.org

[2]

Coon's Log Cabin

Located in Salisbury on the southern Eastern Shore, it shows definite Scandinavian features and is near the intersections of Route 342 and 310. Other log structures are no doubt still hidden in rural areas under plank boards.

Visitor Information

The cabin is used as a vestry house for St. Augustine Episcopal Church and contains a meeting room, Rector's office and Sunday school room.

Coon's Log Cabin
St. Augustine Episcopal Church
PO Box 487
    MD Route 342 (Mitton Rd.) & MD Route 310
    (Cayot's Corner Rd.)
    Chesapeake City MD 21915
phone: 410-885-5375
email: augustineparish@verizon.net
web: augustineparish.org

John Hans Steelman House/Historic Elk Landing

Johan Hanson Steelman (1655-1749) was the oldest son of Hans Månsson and Ella Stille. Born in Pennsylvania at Aronamack (West Philadelphia), he moved to "Sahakito" by 1693 as the foremost Indian trader of the day, living at this site on the Little Elk River. The **stone Steelman house [1]** has now been structurally restored and many Native American implements and trade goods were found in the area.

The actual log house that Johan Hanson Steelman lived in was adjacent to the later stone house and survived until at least 1917. His personal generosity made possible the building of Holy Trinity Church at Christina in 1698-1699 when he provided over one-half of the needed capital. By 1720 he had moved west to what is now Adams County. Here he continued his trading ventures as the first European in that part of the country. The entire Elk Landing site has been protected and developed by the non-profit Historic Elk Landing Foundation that was created in 1998 by the town of Elkton. The large 19th century Hollingsworth mansion is nearby as well as the site of a defeat of British forces during the War of 1812.

[1]

Visitor Information

The houses & grounds are open during festivals, fairs, reenactments and other public events.

John Hans Steelman House/Historic Elk Landing

The Historic Elk Landing Foundation, Inc.

    P.O. Box 277

    590 Landing Lane

    Elkton, Maryland 21922

phone: 410-620-6400

email: info@elklanding.org

web: elklanding.org

Embassy of Sweden

Located where Rock Creek joins the Potomac River, the House of Sweden is much more than an embassy. It is a cultural center, exhibition space and conference locale. In the Georgetown section of Washington, DC, its imposing glass and wood design reflects simplicity, modernity and unpretentious elegance. It was dedicated in October 2006 and is the first permanent location for the embassy. Its Anna Lindh Hall has almost perfect acoustics and its Nobel Hall is the site for many meetings. On the top floor are 19 apartments that have marvelous views of the river. The practicality and flexibility of the design have made the House of Sweden known worldwide. Its designers were Gert Wingård and Tomas Hansen.

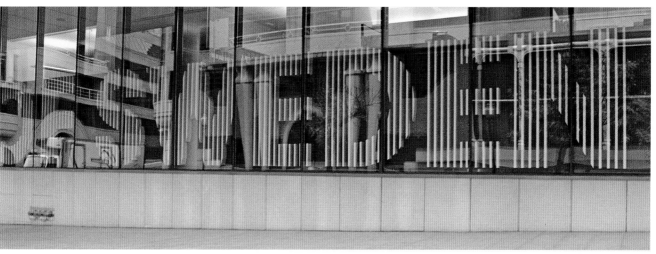

Visitor Information

The building houses the Embassy of Sweden, the
Embassy of Iceland, office suites and an Event Center
that features conference and exhibition halls.

Embassy of Sweden

2900 K Street NW, Washington, DC 20007
phone: 202-467-2600
email: ambassaden.washington@gov.se
web: www.swedenabroad.com/
      en-GB/Embassies/Washington

Embassy of Finland

Just across Massachusetts Avenue from the entrance to the Vice President's residence is the Embassy of Finland. Surrounded by trees, it was erected in 1994. It is an elegant constructivist composition in the spirit of the Finnish architectural giants Saarinen and Aalto. It is the first embassy in this country to receive LEED certification. It is said to be "modest, reserved and quiet" like its people. Yet there is also drama in the building as light pours down from the center of the building through a 60' grand canyon to Finlandia Hall. Besides its ambassadorial functions, it also is a center of Finnish culture and art displays.

Visitor Information

The Embassy of Finland is home to the Finnish – United States relationship, and works to enhance well-being and safety as well as competitiveness, trade and investments in both countries.

Embassy of Finland

3301 Massachusetts Avenue NW, Washington D.C. 20008
phone: 202-298-5800
email: sanomat.was@formin.fi
web: finland.org

The First Hundred Years of the Swedish Colonial Society

In 1888 not many people were aware of the New Sweden Colony, and not many people had done enough genealogy to know that they had New Sweden roots. But the famed Provost of the University of Pennsylvania had taken an interest in his own background from Olof Stille in Roslagen. Charles Janeway Stille visited Sweden, including Penningby Castle in Länna Parish, and arranged to have three volumes of records reproduced and placed in the Historical Society of Pennsylvania, the *Archivum Americanum*. Some Swedish immigrants to the Midwest now realized that they had colonial ancestors on the Delaware. Eight years later the Historical Society of Delaware erected the first ever New Sweden monument at the supposed first site of Holy Trinity Church at Crane Hook, on the south side of the Christina River.

On the tower of Philadelphia's fabulous Beaux Arts City Hall, Alexander Milne Calder placed a statue of a Swedish woman, *Moder Svea*, looking out towards Wicacå, the area of the early Swedish settlers. But it took the arrival of Amandus Johnson, a young Smålänning from Minnesota, to crystallize all of the separate interests in New Sweden. Johnson was his on his way to Yale but stopped in Philadelphia at the University of Pennsylvania and was persuaded to stay and research the New Sweden Colony and teach Swedish at the same time.

After a number of preparatory meetings in 1908, 24 academics and cultural historians gathered in Philadelphia on 20 January 1909 to form the Swedish Colonial Society. The President was to be Marcel A. Viti, Vice Counsel for Sweden in Philadelphia, an Italian who was a great Swedophile and served until 1921 after which he continued as a Councillor until 1953. The Secretary for the next half-century would be Amandus Johnson. The Treasurer and First Vice President was Dr. Gregory B. Keen. He wrote the first constitution and actively sought new members for the Society. By the First Annual Meeting in 1910 there were 201 active men in the Society. No thought was given to women as members, although they were eventually allowed as "associate members" and were called on to staff the "Women's Committee" to take care of banquets. In the beginning it was a men's club that included banquets where one listened to a speaker and then adjourned for "cigars and port." The meetings of the Council were held at the Historical Society of Pennsylvania, which was the official address of the Society. Few meetings lasted more than an hour.

Because the members of the Council consisted of such luminaries as Samuel W. Pennypacker, President of the Historical Society of Pennsylvania; Albert Bushnell Hart, Professor of History at Harvard; Marion D. Learned, Professor of German at the University of Pennsylvania; the Swedish

Ambassador and Consul General from New York; plus Henry A. DuPont and Thomas Francis Bayard; the Council meetings were certainly lively and not easily dominated by one person. It was considered something of a social asset to belong. One of tactics used to increase membership was to consult the *Social Register* in Philadelphia. If many people on the Main Line bragged about arriving on William Penn's *Welcome*, how much better to be able to claim ancestors on the *Kalmar Nyckel*? And it was after all not just a lineage society; anyone with an interest in colonial history was welcome as long as they had a sponsor to bring up their name at a Council meeting.

The Society has always refused to be involved in real estate, except on a temporary basis, and refused to sponsor the American Swedish Historical Museum since it felt that such fund-raising would divert it from its original purpose, much to the chagrin of Amandus Johnson.

The purpose of the organization was stated in the founding documents and has been continued until the present:

> To collect, preserve, and publish records and other documents relating to the history of the Swedes in America.

Note that is was not to be the New Sweden Society, but the Swedish Colonial Society. Its interests were to include all Swedish immigration to the United States. While this wide field has been difficult to cover, except in its archives, the organization soon began to specialize in local Swedish history before the end of the Revolutionary War. It was the first Swedish historical society of any kind in the United States and the first such organization in the Delaware Valley.

The greatest achievements of the Society, in addition to publishing 13 books, are undoubtedly its preservation efforts at Governor Printz Park at Tinicum and at Gloria Dei Church. Both of these major efforts were connected to the charismatic Governor, Colonel Frank Worthington Melvin, who served as President and then Governor for ten years (1936-1946). Indeed, much of what we think of as original traditions of the Society originated with the "Melvin Revolution."

Colonel Melvin, as he was called, was a successful lawyer, and was Chairman of the Pennsylvania Historical Commission for four years. At the same time that he was the Governor of the Society he was also the Chair of the Board of the American Swedish Historical Museum. Certainly a noble feat in itself to hold all three of these positions at once. He re-wrote our Constitution, instituting the present system of officers with a Governor rather than a President. The insignia and Governor's star were introduced. He saw that flags were bought. A "Captain" was elected. The flags were used in super-patriotic ways, e.g. parading in those seated at the head table for a banquet or at a church service. Banquets began with the singing of the national anthems and Colonel Melvin specified a whole series of annual events that could be commemorated in addition to commanding that the three toasts should be with port wine and the food, of whatever type, should be referred to as a smorgasbord! Needless to say, this emphasis on patriotism was not in line with the original purposes of the organization but was useful during World War II when there was skepticism about Sweden's neutrality.

While the annual meetings had been held near April 8th since 1910, usually at the Barclay Hotel, beginning in 1938 they began the format that we use today and call Forefather Luncheons. Beginning in 1977 these luncheons were held alternately with the Delaware Swedish Colonial Society, each Society taking its turn and then having its own dinner on the off years. The Colonial Forefathers Luncheon of 2009 was the first one that had been jointly planned by both Societies in a way that has been continued to the present time.

But as the Chair of the most important State Commission devoted to history, Colonel Melvin was very active. He saw that Pennsbury Manor was recreated, that the Brandywine Battlefield Park was established, that the Morton Homestead was restored, and he wrote all of the legislation concerning the 1938 Jubilee, including the plans to visit Sweden by the Governor of Pennsylvania.

Commodore Charles Longstreth of the Corinthian Yacht Club purchased the Tinicum site in 1922, but nothing had been done to it except that the Society erected a monolith there in 1923. But in 1927, in honor of the transatlantic flight of Charles Lindberg, Charles Longstreth donated the land to the Society. The property was in poor condition, with tumbled down buildings, weeds and an unimproved and very uneven waterfront.

Colonel Melvin saw to it that six projects of the Work Progress Administration were sited there; a sea wall was built, grading completed, trees planted, grass sowed, archeological investigations completed discovering the Printzhof, and some decayed buildings removed. By 1938 it was ready to be given to the Commonwealth of Pennsylvania. In 1972 a heroic statue of Governor Printz by member Carl Lindborg was sited there. In 2003 the state donated the park back to Tinicum Township as an economy move, with the advice of the Society.

By 1942 Colonel Melvin turned his attention to Gloria Dei Church and had it declared a National Historic Landmark – the first church in the country to receive such a designation – and soon after saw to it that the seven acres to the south of the building were added to the site. Gloria Dei is now the legal address of the Society, and its Rector is always ex-officio Chaplain of the Society. When Colonel Melvin retired from the Society he used his experiences at Gloria Dei to help Christ Church in Old City Philadelphia acquire the park land that now faces Market Street.

The *Swedish Colonial News* began in 1990 as an eight-page newsletter and is now a 20-page journal, serving the widely dispersed members in this country and in Sweden. The genealogical program began in 1939 and, under the direction of Dr. Peter S. Craig, has helped more than 350 people discover their New Sweden roots.

The Society's highly successful website, *ColonialSwedes.org* began under the expert leadership of Ronald Hendrickson in 1999 and now has more than 15,000 users each month. After 13 years of remarkable growth it has been redeveloped to include many more historical and genealogical references as well as to make possible book purchases, dues paying and donations on-line. Leif Lundquist in Sweden maintains our sister site, *Nya Sverige I Nord Ameika.se*, for our Scandinavian members in Svenska Colonial Sällskapet. It came on-line in 2009.

The New Sweden History Conference began in 2001 as a joint project between the American Swedish Historical Museum and the Society, bringing together the latest research about New Sweden, in co-operation with the McNeil Center for Early American Studies at the University of Pennsylvania. The Delaware Swedish Colonial Society, the New Sweden Centre, the Kalmar Nyckel Foundation and Trinity Church, Swedesboro are now co-sponsors for this annual event in the autumn.

The Archives program hosted at the Lutheran Archives Center in Philadelphia began in 2000 with the work of Kim-Eric Williams and now amounts to more than 42 linear feet of institutional and cultural materials, a map collection and framed paintings, including a fabulous large copy of the 17th century Botnaryd Church portrait of Governor Printz, given to the Society by King Gustaf V in 1910. The painting is especially important since, before it arrived from the King, no one in America had any idea how Johan Printz appeared. The Archives collection has more than doubled since the acquisition of the Craig and Rambo collections of genealogical materials. It now comprises the largest printed collection of New Sweden materials in existence. Most of its genealogical materials are currently being made available on the Society's website, thanks to the enormous work of Ronald S. Beatty and the Rev. Dr. Cynthia Forde-Beatty, Society genealogists.

As early as 1946, women began to be more active with the first two women elected to the Council, Sarah Logan Wister Starr and A. Florence Appleberg

Ingle. In the same year the first woman officer, Miss Gladys Peterson became the Recording Secretary. She served for 40 years. We have revised the By-laws twice in the past five years to eliminate all sexist references and to make the officers' duties more precise. In Margaret Sooy Bridwell we have our first woman Governor. Before her, the highest rank that any woman had attained was Senior Deputy Governor when the Countess Waterman-Gherilli was elected to that office, but never became Governor. The position of Junior Deputy Governor was ably filled by Esther Ann MacFarland beginning in 1993. The glass ceiling has now finally been breached.

The Society also was active in other ways: in the 1926 Sesquicentennial National Exhibition in Philadelphia with a model of the Wicacå blockhouse, in the 1988 350th Celebration of New Sweden and in the 1993 celebration of 350 years of government in Pennsylvania. Its members supported the formation of the Amercian Swedish Historical Museum, the Delaware Swedish Colonial Society, the Kalmar Nyckel Foundation, and the New Sweden Centre. The Society endowed an "Amandus Johnson Prize" at the University of Pennsylvania that is a travel grant to study in Sweden for one who excels in language study. It assisted with the New Sweden Heritage Monument erection in New Jersey. The Rambo Apple Friendship Project, under the direction of Honorary Governor Herbert R. Rambo and Councillor Hans Ling of Uppsala, Sweden has spread the word about the New Sweden Colony all over the country and in selected areas of Sweden. Although the Rambo apple tree had become extinct in Sweden since 1708, by heroic efforts it was re-introduced in ways that gave us the ability to tell the forgotten story of New Sweden. The Society has also acted as a resource for the proposed National Park in Delaware and with the establishment of a World Heritage UNESCO Linnean site at Bartram's Garden. It is now supporting the redevelopment of the Swedish Farmstead outdoor museum in Bridgeton, NJ.

In this year, 2013, the sixth volume of *Colonial Records of Swedish Churches in Pennsylvania* will come off the press and perhaps one or two more volumes will complete the set, bringing the records up to the installation of the last Swedish pastor at Gloria Dei, Nils Collin. A joint planning committee has been established for all of the Swedish groups in the Delaware Valley to coordinate the events regarding the 375th Jubilee of New Sweden this year.

Kim-Eric Williams
Honorary Governor
Archivist

Forefather's Luncheon
29 March 2009

Revised July 2010 and December 2012
West Chester, PA

Governors
of the
Swedish
Colonial Society
1909 – present

33. Margaret Sooy Bridwell, 2010-

32. Herbert R. Rambo, 2009-2010

31. The Rev. Kim-Eric Williams, D.Min., 2005-2009

30. Ronald A. Hendrickson, Esq., 2003-2005

29. Herbert R. Rambo, 2000-2003

28. William Benjamin Neal, 1997-2000

27. Commander John W. Widfeldt, 1995-1997

26. John C. Cameron, Esq., 1993-1995

25. Wallace F. Richter, 1989-1993

24. Dr. Erik G.M. Tornqvist, 1986-1989

23. Benkt Wennberg, Ph.D., 1984-1986

22. Herbert E. Hanson Gullberg, 1982-1984

21. Dr. Erik G.M. Tornqvist, 1977-1982

20. David Hillman, 1975-1977

19. The Rev. John Craig Roak, D.D., 1972-1975

18. Conrad Wilson, 1970-1972

17. Allen Lesley, Esq., 1968-1970

16. Donald E. Hogeland, Esq., 1966-1968

15. Charles Paist, III, 1964-1966

14. Alan Corson, Jr., 1962-1964

13. C. Colket Wilson, Jr., 1960-1962

12. Amandus Johnson, Ph.D., 1958-1960

11. Samuel Booth Sturgis, M.D., 1956-1958

10. Frederic Swing Crispin, 1954-1956

9. Colonel Robert Morris, 1952-1954

8. Issac Crawford Sutton, Esq., 1950-1952

7. Charles Sinnickson, Esq., 1948-1950

6. Branton Holstein Henderson, 1946-1948

5. Col. Frank W. Melvin, Esq., 1936-1946

4. Albert Duncan Yocum, Ph.D., 1932-1936

3. Colonel Henry D. Paxson, Esq., 1927-1932

2. Gregory B. Keen, L.L.D., 1921-1927

1. The Honorable Marcel A. Viti, 1909-1921

The title was changed from President to Governor in 1944.

Publications of the
Swedish Colonial Society

www.ColonialSwedes.org

On the internet since 1999, a web site featuring news and information about the New Sweden Colony in America.

Swedish Colonial News

Twice-yearly since 1990, a 20-page news magazine of New Sweden history, genealogy and current events.

Colonial Records of the Swedish Churches in Pennsylvania

By Peter Stebbins Craig – Editor,
and Kim-Eric Williams – Assistant Editor & Translator

Volume 5: The Parlin Years, 1750-1759

Volume 4: From Lidman to Näsman, 1719-1750

Volume 3: The Sandel Years, 1702-1719

Volume 2: The Rudman Years, 1697-1702

Volume 1: The Log Churches at Tinicum Island and Wicaco, 1646-1696

The Faces of New Sweden:
Erik Björk, Christina Stalcop & America's First Portrait Painter
by Hans Ling
2004 - 104 pages and 17 color images.

365th Jubilee Celebration -
New Sweden: Past, Present and Future
by Ronald A. Hendrickson, Esq.
2003 - 16 pages and 16 color images.

Swedish Contributions to
American Freedom, 1776-1783
by Amandus Johnson, Ph.D.
1953 & 1957 - two volumes, 1,184 pages,
50 illustrations and two maps.

The Naval Campaigns of
Count de Grasse During the
American Revolution, 1781-1783
by Carl Gustaf Törnqvist
translation and additional material
by Amandus Johnson, Ph.D.
1942 - 204 pages, seven illustrations
and eight naval plans.

The Instruction for Johan Printz,
Governor of New Sweden
translation and additional material
by Amandus Johnson, Ph.D.
1930 - 303 pages, 24 illustrations and one map.

Where Pennsylvania History Began
by Henry D. Paxson
1926

Geographia Americae, or
a Description of Indiae Occidentalis
by Per Lindeström
translation and additional material
by Amandus Johnson, Ph.D.
1925 - 462 pages, 43 illustrations,
eight maps and documents.

The Swedes on the Delaware, 1638-1664
by Amandus Johnson, Ph.D.
1915 - 391 pages and 34 illustrations.

Johan Classon Rising,
The Last Governor of New Sweden
by Amandus Johnson, Ph.D.
1915 - 16 pages and one illustration.

The Descendants of
Jöran Kyn of New Sweden
by Gregory B. Keen, LL.D.
1913 - 318 pages and one map.

The Swedish Settlements on
the Delaware, 1638-1664
by Amandus Johnson, Ph.D.
1911 - two volumes, 899 pages,
167 illustrations and six maps.

In addition to the above major works, the Society
has issued numerous publications of Society history
and proceedings.

A Guide to New Sweden Forefathers, 1638–1664 Arrivals

by Dr. Peter Stebbins Craig
Fellow, American Society of Genealogists
Fellow, Genealogical Society of Pennsylvania
Historian, Swedish Colonial Society

originally published in *Swedish Colonial News*,
Volume 1, Number 18 (Fall 1999)

Surname	Immigrant	Died
Anderson (MD)	Måns Andersson	MD 1680
Anderson (DE)	Anders Andersson the Finn	DE 1673+
Anderson (DE)	Anders Jöransson	DE 1675
Archer (PA-NJ)	Johan Grelsson	PA 1684
Bankson/Bankston (PA)	Anders Bengtsson	PA 1705
Bartleson, Andrew (PA-NJ)	Bärtil Eskilsson	PA 1677+
Bilderback (NJ)	Hendrick Johansson	DE 1655+
Block (DE)	Hans Block*	DE 1676
Boatsman (DE)	Jöran Jöransson Båtsman	DE 1691
Boon(PA-NJ)	Anders Svensson Bonde	PA 1696
Boyer (DE)	Alexander Boyer*	DE 1661+
Bure (PA)	Lars Thomasson Bjur	PA 1658+
Calk/Caulk (MD)	Olof Matthiasson Isgrå	MD 1685
Camp/Kemp (MD-NJ)	Pål Larsson Kämpe	MD 1692
Classon/Clawson (PA-DE)	Claes Johansson	DE 1655+
Clementson/Clements	Clement Jöranasson	DE 1648+
Coleman (PA-NJ)	Anders Hendricksson	PA 1655+
Cock/Cox (PA-NJ-DE)	Peter Larsson Cock	PA 1687
Cock/Cox (PA)	Otto Ernest Koch*	PA 1722
Cock/Cox (DE)	Anders Andersson the Finn	DE 1673+
Constantine (DE)	Constantine Grönenberg	DE 1657+
Corneliuson (NJ)	Lars Cornelisson Vinarn	NJ 1686
Culin/van Culin	Johan van Culin*	PA 1711
Dalbo (NJ)	Anders Larsson Dalbo	PA 1670

Surname	Immigrant	Died
Danielson (NJ)	Hendrick Danielsson	NJ 1695+
Defoss (DE)	Matthias Mattsson de Vos	DE 1708
Derickson (NJ-DE)	Eric Michaelsson	PA 1663+
Eareckson (MD)	Johan Ericksson	MD 1674
Enochs/Enochson (PA)	Garret Enochson*	PA 1681+
Erickson (NJ)	Eric Michaelsson	PA 1663+
Erickson (DE)	Eric Mattsson	DE 1671+
Evertson (DE)	Ivert Hendricksson	DE 1684
Fish (NJ)	Johan Fisk alias Skofvel	DE 1655+
Franson (NJ)	Olof Fransson	NJ 1700
Friend (PA-NJ-MD)	Nils Larsson Frände	PA 1686
Garrett (PA)	Mårten Gerritsen	DE 1680
Gästenberg (PA)	Olof Nilsson Gästenberg	PA 1692
Halton (NJ)	Jöns Jönsson	PA 1658+
Hanson (MD)	Anders Hansson	MD 1655
Helm (NJ)	Israel Åkesson Helm	NJ 1701
Hendrickson (PA-NJ)	Johan Hendricksson	PA 1657+
Hendrickson (DE)	Hendrick Larsson Corvhorn	DE 1693+
Hendrickson (DE)	Hendrick Andersson	DE 1696
Hendrickson (DE-NJ)	Hendrick Jacobsson	DE 1704
Hendrickson (MD)	Hendrick Hendricksson	MD 1679+
Hendrickson (MD)	Bärtil Hendricksson	MD 1684
Hoffman (NJ)	Hans Hopman*	NJ 1693
Holstein/Holston (PA-NJ)	Matthias Claessen Holstein*	PA 1708
Homan (NJ)	Anders Andersson Homman	NJ 1700
Huling (PA-NJ)	Marcus Laurenson*	NJ 1689
Johnson (PA)	Claes Johansson	DE 1655+
Johnson (PA)	Johan Hendricksson	PA 1657+
Johnson (PA-NJ)	Anders Jönsson Salung	PA 1687
Johnson (MD)	Peter Johansson	MD 1656
Johnson (MD)	Simon Johansson	MD 1700+
Johnson (NJ-MD)	Matthias Jönsson Hutt	NJ 1685
Jonason/Jones (PA)	Jonas Nilsson	PA 1693
Jones (NJ)	Anders Jönsson Ekoren	PA 1683
Justice/Justis (PA-DE)	Johan Gustafsson	PA 1682
Justice/Justison (NJ)	Jöns Gustafsson	NJ 1698+

Surname	Immigrant	Died
Justison (DE)	Pål Persson	PA 1663+
Keen (DE-NJ)	Jürgen Schneeweiss Kühn	PA 1688+
King (NJ-DE)	Frederick Fredericksson König*	NJ 1698
Kuckow (NJ-DE)	Olof Olleson Kucko	DE 1696
Litien (NJ)	Eric Jöransson	NJ 1685
Lykins/Likins (PA)	Peter Nilsson Lykan	PA 1692
Lykins/Likins (NJ)	Michael Nilsson Lykan	NJ 1704
Lock (NJ)	Lars Carlsson Lock	PA 1688
Longacre (PA)	Peter Andersson	PA 1678
Lom (PA)	Måns Svensson Lom	PA 1653
Matthiasson (MID)	Hendrick Matthiasson Freeman	MD 1685
Matson (DE)	Johan Mattsson Skrika	DE 1691
Mattson (NJ)	Matts Hansson	PA 1653
Mink (NJ)	Pål Pålsson Mink	NJ 1696
Morton (PA-NJ)	Mårten Mårtensson	PA 1706
Morton (PA)	Knut Mårtensson	PA 1677+
Månsson/Mounts (DE)	Måns Pålsson	DE 1682
Mounts (MD)	Måns Andersson	MD 1680
Mullica (NJ)	Pål Jönsson Mullica	DE 1664
Nelson (NJ)	Nils Mattsson	PA 1701
Nelson (NJ)	Nils Nilsson	DE 1670
Numbers (MD)	Johan Nommersson	MD 1697+
Parker (DE-MD)	Peter Hendricksson	DE 1684
Paulson (DE)	Pål Persson	PA 1663+
Paulson (NJ)	Pål Larsson Corvhorn	NJ 1688
Paulson (MD)	Pål Jönsson Mullica	DE 1664
Peterson (DE)	Samuel Petersson	DE 1689
Peterson (DE)	Matthias Eskilsson	DE 1671+
Peterson (DE)	Hans Petersen*	DE 1720
Peterson (MD)	Peter Jacobsson	MD 1674
Peterson (MD)	Peter Månsson	MD 1682
Peterson (NJ)	Peter Ollesson	NJ 1691
Peterson (NJ)	Lucas Petersson	NJ 1686
Peterson (PA-NJ)	Måns Petersson Stake	PA 1697
Peterson (NJ)	Hans Petersson	NJ 1693
Rambo (PA-NJ)	Peter Gunnarsson Rambo	PA 1698
Rawson (PA-DE-MD)	Olof Rase/Rawson	PA 1697

Surname	Immigrant	Died
Scoggin (NJ)	Johan Thorsson Schaggen	DE 1658
Severson (MD)	Marcus Sigfridsson	MD 1674+
Sinex/Sinnickson (PA-NJ)	Sinnick Broer	DE 1673
Skute/Scuten (PA)	Sven Svensson Skute	PA 1660+
Slubey (NJ-DE-MD)	Olof from Slobyn	PA 1671+
Snicker (MD)	Jöran Jönsson	DE 1677
Stalcup/Stallcup (DE)	Johan Anderson Stålkofta	DE 1684
Stark (NJ)	Nils Nilsson	DE 1670
Steelman(NJ)	Hans Månsson	NJ 1691
Stidham/Stedham (DE)	Timen Stiddem	DE 1686
Stille/Stilley (PA-DE)	Olof Petersson Stille	PA 1683
String (NJ)	Johan Anderson Sträng	NJ 1726
Swanson (PA)	Sven Gunnarsson	PA 1678
Thomason/Thompson (DE-PA)	Thomas Jacobsson	DE 1679+
Tolson (MD)	Alexander Thorsson	MD 1669
Tolson (MD)	Anders Thorsson	MD 1671+
Torton (PA)	Hendrick Tade	PA 1703
Toy (NJ-PA)	Elias Johnson Tay	NJ 1720
Tussey (DE)	Olof Thorsson	DE 1678
Urian (PA-NJ)	Hans Geörgen*	PA 1713
Vandever(DE)	Catharina Johansdotter**	NJ 1720
Vinam/Vining (NJ-MD)	Lars Cornelisson Vinam	NJ 1686
Walraven (DE)	Christina Ollesdotter**	DE 1699
Wheeler (MD-PA)	John Wheeler	MD 1677
Woolson (NJ)	Hans Ollesson	NJ 1702+
Yocum/Yocom (PA)	Peter Jochimsson	PA 1654

Settlers having Daughters Only

Matthias Bärtilsson, NJ 1680

Mats Bengtsson, PA 1662

Hendrick Andersson Coleman, PA 1697

Gustaf Danielsson, PA 1681

Johan Erickson, NJ 1691

Gotfried Harmer, MD 1674

Lars Hendricksson, NJ 1687

Carl Jönsson, PA 1683

Hendrick Lemmens, DE 1687

Matthias Matthiasson, NJ 1678

Olof Philipsson, PA 1656+

Lars Svensson, PA 1651

Jacob Jongh (Young), PA 1686

*Married to Swedish wives   **Married to Dutch husbands

Index

New Sweden Forefathers are listed on pages 118 - 121.
Governors of the Swedish Colonial Society are listed on page 115.

Vaino Aaltonen 49
ABBA 8
Israel Acrelius..24, 53
Algonquin 13, 48
American Swedish Historical Museum 37, 42,
                                       43, 44, 45, 69, 111, 113, 114
Amity Township 66
Ammansland..33, 53
David Anderson 11
Anglican...66, 96
Annapolis 95
Queen Anne 97
A. Florence Appleberg..113
Archivum Americanum 110
Aronamack 100
Atlantic City 93
Augustana Institute 69
Jonas Aurén 96, 97
University of Åbo (Turku) 75

Barclay Hotel 112
John Bartram 60
William Bartram 60
Bartram's Garden 60, 61, 114
Bastu 13
Bayard family 25
Thomas Francis Bayard 111
Ronald S. Beatty...113
Paula Himmelsbach Belano 64
Lord Berkeley 71
Berks County 66, 68
Prince Bertil 21
Erik Björk 22, 24
Black Anthony 21
Boon family..53
Bottnaryd Church 113
Benjamin Braman...80
Brandywine Battlefield Park 112
Brandywine River..19
Fredrika Bremer...41
Bridgeport 64
Bridgeton 88, 114
Margaret Sooy Bridwell 11, 114
Brossman Center 69
Daniel Paul Bryzelius 90

Calcon Hook 33, 53
Alexander Milne Calder 46, 110
Calvert family 95

Johan Campanius 48, 97
Sir George Carteret 71
Chester 33, 48, 49
Christ Church 113
Christ Church Upper Merion 64, 65
Queen Christina 39
Christina River 15, 22, 28, 83, 95, 100, 110
Church of Sweden 22, 24, 39, 40, 95
Cinnaminson (Senamensing) 71
Civil Works Administration 86
Jehu Curtis Clay 40
Claymont..29
Claymont Historical Society 29
Nicholas (Nils) Collin..40, 75, 114
Colonial Dames of America 63
Colonial Records of Swedish Churches in
        Pennsylvania 114
ColonialSwedes.org 5, 113
Conestoga 97
Constitution 15
Coon's Log Cabin 99
Corinthian Yacht Club 36, 112
Peter Craig 11, 113
Craig Collection 69, 113
Crane Hook...22, 28, 110
Crum Creek 26
Cumberland County Historical Society...............................89

Dala-Floda 88
Darby Creek 50, 52, 57
Declaration of Independence 8, 42, 48
Delaware Bay 5
Delaware Memorial Bridge 28, 84
Delaware River 5, 8, 11, 26, 29, 30, 33, 36, 39, 71, 84, 92, 96
Delaware Swedish Colonial Society 25, 26, 112, 113, 114
Delaware Valley 8, 11, 13, 15, 33, 60, 63, 69, 111, 114
Delmarva Peninsula 95
Denmark 17
Douglassville...66
Drexel Hill...57
DuPont 19
Henry A. DuPont 111

Elk Landing 100, 101
Elk River 95, 100
Elkton 96, 100
Elliott family 25
Elsinboro...73
Elvsborg 73

Embassy of Finland 106, 107, 108, 109
Embassy of Sweden 102, 103, 104, 105
Episcopal 90
John Ericsson 8
Essington 33

Jacob Fabritius 39
Gabriel Falk 66
Falun 27
John Fenwick 71
Finland 5, 9, 49, 75
Finlandia Hall 106
Finn's Point 71, 83
First State 15
Fogel Grip 9, 15, 40
Cynthia Forde-Beatty 113
Forest Finns 13
Fort Casimir 30, 73
Fort Christina 13, 15, 20, 21, 22, 28, 33
Fort Elfsborg 30, 72, 73
Fort Trinity 31
Friends of the Swedish Log Cabin 57
Friesburg 93

Gabriel 41
King George I 83
Georgetown 102
Lars Girelius 24
Gloria Dei (Old Swedes') Church 31, 38, 39, 40, 41, 46, 48, 58, 64, 66, 74, 111, 112, 113, 114
Gloucester County Historical Society 77
Gothenburg 15, 17, 21, 73
Grand Sprute Plantation 77
Great Copper Mining Company 27
Great Egg Harbor 93
Greenwich 89
King Gustaf Adolf 21
King Gustaf II Adolf 15
King Gustaf V 27, 113

Jonas Hafström 8
Haga Royal Palace 69
Sarah Hancock 86
William Hancock 86
Hancock House 86
Tomas Hansen 102
Harrisburg 33, 37
Albert Bushnell Hart 110
Harvard University 110
Israel Helm 80
Maria Helm 66
Helsinki 74
Anders Hendrickson 26
Nancy Hendrickson 11
Ronald Hendrickson 11, 113
Hendrickson House 26, 27, 28
Gustavus Hesselius 29
Historic Elk Landing Foundation 100
Historical Society of Delaware 28, 110

Historical Society of Pennsylvania 110
Aleasa Hogate 11
Hollingsworth Mansion 100
Holstein family 64
Holy Trinity (Old Swedes') Church 22, 23, 24, 25, 26, 28, 39, 74, 100, 110
Caesar Hoskins Log Cabin 92

Immanuel Episcopal Church 31
Independence National Historical Park 39, 75

King James II 71
Amandus Johnson 42, 110, 111
Måns Jonasson 60, 68

Pehr Kalm 60, 74
Kalmar 17
Kalmar Nyckel 8, 9, 15, 16, 17, 18, 20, 40, 111, 113, 114
Gregory B. Keen 110
Kingsessing 33, 53
Koores 13
Ritva Koukku-Ronde 9

Stieg Larsson 8
Lear/Mårtenson Log Cabin 77
Marion D. Learned 110
Lenape 13, 15, 20, 46, 84, 97
Lenapehocking 13
Lewes 17
Jenny Lind 41
Charles Lindberg 112
Carl Lindborg 36, 112
Astrid Lindgren 8
Anna Lindh Hall 102
Lindsborg 69
Hans Ling 114
Carl Linnaeus 60
Lars Carlson Lock 22, 28
Log cabin 9
Pippi Longstocking 8
Charles Longstreth 112
Lower Counties 15
Lower Swedish Log Cabin 56, 57
Lucia Fest 25
Leif Lundquist 113
Lutheran Archives Center 69, 113
Lutheran Theological Seminary 69
Länna Parish 110

Esther Ann MacFarland 114
Malcolm Mackenzie 18
Main Line 111
Manatawny 66
Mantua Creek 71
Mason-Dixon survey 95
Maurice River 74, 91, 92, 93
McNeil Center for Early American Studies 113
Frank Worthington Melvin 111, 112, 113
Methodist 92

Mill Creek 53
Mill Valley 62
Millennium Trilogy 8
Carl Milles 20, 40
Minquis River 15
Peter Minuit 9, 13, 15, 95
Monitor 8
Monument to Finnish Settlers 49
Mt. Airy 69
Moravian 74, 92
Moravian Church on Oldman's Creek 90
Moravian Church Site on Maurice River 91
Moravian Historical Society 90
John Morton 8, 42, 48, 50, 52
Morton Homestead 50, 51, 112
Morton Morton 52
Morton Morton House 52
Mouns Jones House 68
Mountain Laurel (*Kalmia Multiflora*) 60
Muckinipattus Creek 52
Eric Mullica 75, 78
John Mullica 78
William Mullica 79
Mullica Hill 78
Mullica House 78, 79
Munsi 13
Hans Månsson 100
Birgitta Mårtenson 26
Matthias Mårtenson 50
Mårten Mårtenson 48, 77
Mölndahl 62

Naaman's Creek 29
Netherlands 17
New Amstel 31
New Castle 15, 17, 28, 30, 31, 73
New Gothenburg 33
New Haven 71
New Netherland 15, 30
New Stockholm 71
New Sweden Centre 18, 28, 113, 114
New Sweden Colonial Farmstead Museum
   & Living History Center 88, 114
New Sweden Colony 5, 13, 39, 46, 49, 64, 69,
                          78, 85, 88, 95, 97, 110, 113, 114
New Sweden Company 15, 19, 33
New Sweden Heritage Monument 84, 114
New Sweden History Conference 113
New Sweden Park 77
New Sweden Society 111
Alfred Nobel 8
Nobel Hall 102
Nobel Prizes 8
Nordic Museum 63
Norfolk 17
North East 96
Norwood 52
Norwood Historical Society 52
C.A. Nothnagle Log House 80, 81

Nya Sverige I Nord Ameika.se 113

Oklahoma 13
Old Morlatton Village 68
Old Swedes Foundation 26
Old Swedish Burial Ground 48
Oldman's Creek 74, 90
Ontario 13
Prince Oscar 64

Paradise Point 5
Paulsboro 80
William Penn 11, 15, 33, 46, 66, 71, 111
Penningby Castle 110
Pennsbury Manor 112
Pennsville 71, 74, 83, 90, 91
Pennsylvania Historical and Museum
   Commission 37, 50, 111, 112
University of Pennsylvania 110, 113, 114
Samuel W. Pennypacker 110
Peterson family 53
Gladys Peterson 114
Kenneth Peterson 11
Philadelphia 15, 29, 31, 39, 46, 47, 48, 63, 66,
                          69, 74, 75, 110, 111, 113, 114
Philadelphia Museum of Art 29
Port Elizabeth 74, 92
Potomac River 102
Price family 25
Price's Corner 21
Johan Printz 20, 33, 36, 37, 63, 71, 73, 95, 112, 113
Johan Printz Park Log Cabin 85, 111
Printz's (Old Swedes') Mill at Cobbs Creek 62, 63
Printzhof 33, 37, 112
Prospect Park 50
Provincetown 17
Provincial Assembly 15

Quaker 11, 15, 33, 60, 71, 87
Queen's Village 39

Raccoon Creek 74, 77, 78
Herbert Rambo 11, 114
Peter Gunnarson Rambo 69
Rambo Apple Friendship Project 69, 114
Rambo Apple Tree 60, 69
Rambo Collection 69, 113
Rambo family 64
Raritan River 13
Rautalampi 49
Reading 66
Torkil Reorus 22
Repaupo 71
Revolutionary War 8, 15, 39, 75, 111
Ridley Creek 54
Ridley Township 33
Johan Rising 26, 30
Riverview Beach Park 84
Andrew Robeson 66, 80

Robyn 8
Rock Creek 102
The Rocks 15, 17, 20, 49, 95
Franklin D. Roosevelt.............................21, 42
Roslagen 110
Royal Agricultural University 60
Andreas Rudman 31, 40, 41, 66
Ellen Rye 11

Sahakito 100
St. Gabriel's Episcopal Church 66, 67
St. George's Episcopal (Old Swedes') Church 82, 83
St. James Church of Kingsessing................48, 58, 59
St. Mary Anne's Episcopal Church 96, 97, 98
St. Mary's 95, 96
St. Paul's Church 48
Salem 71, 85, 86, 93
Salem Nuclear Generating Station 73
Salem River..73
Salisbury 99
Marcus Samuelson 8
Andreas Sandel 40
Johan Sandin 74
Sauna 13
Schorn Log Cabin...77
Schuylkill River 64, 66
Doriney Seagers 11
James Seagers 11
Senoares 13
Earl Seppala 11
Sylvia Seppala..11
Serpentinite 84
Sesquicentennial National Exhibition.........114
John Sharples 54
Joseph Sharpless 54
Smithsonian Institution 97
Social Register 111
Society of Colonial Dames 46
Annika Sorenstam 8
South River 15, 33
Charles Springer..25
Stalcop-Fenimore log cabin 21
Sarah Logan Wister Starr 113
Steelman (Stille) Family Cemetery................93
John Hans Steelman House 100, 101
Timen Stiddem Mill Site.................................19
Stidham family 19, 25
Charles Janeway Stille 110
Ella Stille...100
John Stille 54
Olof Stille 54, 110
Wolley Stille 54
Stockholm...63
Peter Stuyvesant 30
Pia Sundhagen 8
Sveaborg 74, 83
Jesper Svedberg 74
Svenska Colonial Sällskapet 113
Sweat lodge 13

Sweden 5, 8, 9, 13, 15, 20, 21, 64, 66, 69,
74, 83, 110, 112, 113, 114
Swedes Town 96
Swedesboro 74, 78, 83, 90, 91, 92, 93
Swedesburg 64
Swedish Colonial News 113
Swedish Colonial Society 5, 9, 11, 18, 21, 33,
36, 39, 42, 46, 58, 63, 69, 110, 111, 112, 113, 114
Swedish Council of America 11
Swedish Granary 89

Techoherassi: Olof Stille Site..................54, 55
10 Öre Collection 20
Tinicum Island 33, 36, 37, 39, 48, 50, 53, 111, 112
Lars Tollstadius 74
Peter Tranberg 24
Trinity Chapel..23
Trinity Episcopal (Old Swedes') Church 74, 75, 76, 77, 113
Turkey Point 53
John Tyler 87
Tyler (Hancock) Log House.........................86, 87

UNESCO World Heritage Linnean site 60, 114
Union flag 64
Upland...33, 48, 49
Upper Darby 57
Upper Log Cabin 57
Uppsala 114
Urian family 53

Vandeveer family 25
Varkens Kill..71
Crown Princess Victoria.................................75
Marcel A. Viti 110
Västervik...64

Raoul Wallenberg 8
War Between the States...................................8
George Washington 29
Washington, DC 102
Countess Waterman-Gherilli 114
Welcome 111
Adolf Ulrich Wertmuller.................................29
Wertmuller House 29
Wicacå...39, 46, 110, 114
Kim-Eric Williams.............................11, 113, 114
Thomas Willing 15
Willingtown...15
Wilmington 9, 15, 19, 49, 96
Gert Wingård 102
Work Progress Administration 112
Carl Magnus Wrangel 58

Yale University 110
Yocum family 64

Gunnar Zetterquist.....................................85, 88

Editor

Ronald A. Hendrickson, Esq., is the editor of *New Sweden on the Delaware*. He is a descendant of eight New Sweden settlers, most notably his 10th great-grandfather *Johan Hendricksson*, who arrived with his family on the vessel *Eagle* in 1654. His 8th great-grandfather built the "Hendrickson House" which was reconstructed in 1959 at Holy Trinity (Old Swedes') Church in Wilmington. He is a Fellow of the Swedish Colonial Society, served as Governor from 2003-2005 and, for service in the Swedish-American community, in 2006 Hendrickson was knighted by King Carl XVI Gustaf of Sweden.

Design

The artists of **Cataleno & Company – Nancy Cataleno, Ron Hendrickson, José Ramirez** and **Rose Dominiano –** have designed most of the publications for the Swedish Colonial Society in the modern era.

In 1998, Cataleno revised the layout of *Swedish Colonial News* and expanded its coverage to 20 pages. Since then, this twice-yearly news magazine has become a primary source for New Sweden history, genealogy and current events.

A year later, the designers saw a need for an electronic presence and created the Society's web site at *www.ColonialSwedes.org*. The staff at Cataleno served as webmasters from 1999 to 2009 for the web site that contained 300+ pages and reached viewers worldwide.

To celebrate the 365th Jubilee, in 2003 Cataleno & Company designed and produced the commemorative materials, including the booklet *New Sweden: Past, Present and Future*.

The monograph *The Faces of New Sweden: Erik Björk, Christina Stalcop & America's First Portrait Painter* was designed in 2004 to celebrate the discovery and restoration of the paintings of these important colonial ancestors.

Photography

Kenneth S. Peterson is the son of Stanley and Anna Peterson of Stratford, Camden County, New Jersey. He is a Fellow, Forefather Member and former Junior Deputy Governor, Archivist and Marshal of the Swedish Colonial Society. Kenneth is a descendant of Måns Petersson Stake and wife Magdalentje Lamberts Van Tellickhuysen; their son Peter Peterson and Anna Fish, his wife; Måns Lom and his daughter Anna and her husband Gustaf Danielsson; Johan Fisk and his son Caspar Fisk and his wife Margaret Danielsson; and Peter Nilsson Lycon.

Kenneth contributes to the publications *Swedish Colonial News* and the *Colonial Records of the Swedish Churches in Pennsylvania*. His works include "Måns Petersson Stake of New Sweden and his son Peter Peterson of Maurice River, New Jersey"; "Henry Jacobs Falkinburg" and "Historical Quotations on Swedish Fort Elfsborg". He also created an extensive collection of replica historical maps of New Sweden and the colonial Delaware Valley.

Kenneth S. Peterson is an Industrial Specialist for the U.S. Navy at Lakehurst, New Jersey, specializing in Aircraft Launch and Recovery Equipment. His home is in Whiting, Ocean County, New Jersey. Kenneth lives with his wife, Barbara Bettler and their daughter, Christina Peterson. He has two older daughters, Erika and Katherine.

Text

Kim-Eric Williams was born, and now again resides, in West Chester, Pennsylvania. He graduated from Muhlenberg College in Allentown, Pennsylvania (AB), the Lutheran Theological Seminary in Gettysburg, Pennsylvania (MDiv) and the Graduate Theological Foundation in Notre Dame, Indiana (DMin). As an ordained Lutheran pastor, he served churches in New Jersey, Connecticut, Trinidad and Sweden. He is currently Swedish Lecturer at the University of Pennsylvania, Archivist at the Lutheran Archives Center at Philadelphia, Archivist of the Southeastern Pennsylvania Synod - ELCA, Curator of the Augustana Museum at the Lutheran Seminary in Philadelphia, one of the editors and major translator of the multi-volume series *Colonial Records of Swedish Churches in Pennsylvania*, and Historian of the Swedish Colonial Society.

Kim-Eric is an Honorary Governor of the Swedish Colonial Society and a Fellow of the Society. He became a Knight of the Royal North Star Order from King Carl XVI Gustaf in 2007. On his mother's Talley side of the family, he is descended from at least three New Sweden families: Olof Stille (1641), Hendrick Jacobsson (1654) and Carl Springer (1679). His daughters Lovisa and Pia live in Virginia and his son Justin and daughter Sarah live in Connecticut.

He has published numerous articles and essays including a biography of the first Lutheran pastor ordained in America, *The Journey of Justus Falckner* (ALPB Books, Delhi, NY, 2003)